the secret language of
the soul

the secret language of
the soul

a visual key to
the spiritual world

Jane Hope

CHRONICLE BOOKS

SAN FRANCISCO

The Secret Language of the Soul
Jane Hope

This edition first published in the United States in 2003
by Chronicle Books LLC.

Conceived, edited and designed by Duncan Baird Publishers Ltd.,
Sixth Floor, Castle House, 75–76 Wells Street, London W1T 3QH

First published in Great Britain in 1997 by Mitchell Beazley.

Editor: Joanne Clay
Designer: Gail Jones
Managing Editor: Christopher Westhorp
Managing Designer: Manisha Patel
Commissioned Artwork: Alison Barret, Matthew Cooper,
    Hannah Firmin, Louisa St Pierre
Picture Researcher: Cecilia Weston-Baker
Cover Design: Benjamin Shaykin

Library of Congress Cataloging-in-Publication Data available.

ISBN 0-8118-3822-6

Distributed in Canada by Raincoast Books
9050 Shaughnessy Street
Vancouver, BC V6P 6E5

10 9 8 7 6 5 4 3 2

Chronicle Books LLC
85 Second Street
San Francisco, California 94105
www.chroniclebooks.com

Main text typeset in Garamond
Colour reproduction by Colourscan, Singapore
Manufactured in Singapore

NOTES
The abbreviations BCE and CE are used throughout this book:
BCE Before the Common Era (the equivalent of BC)
CE Common Era (the equivalent of AD)

CONTENTS

Contents

INTRODUCTION

Throughout the ages, belief in an inner "soul" or "spirit" has contributed a unique and valuable dimension to human life. The soul is invisible – a vital essence that breathes existence into humanity and the natural world. Our awareness of the spiritual is intuitive, achieved through a deep instinct that speaks to us of the interconnectedness of all living things. It is the soul that informs the compassion we feel for others and that suffuses the mundane with a sense of the sacred. It is the soul that translates incident into experience, knowledge into wisdom.

The subject of this book is the language of the soul or spirit, which has usually been expressed in enigmatic form – it could not have been otherwise, for profound truths accessible through imagination, religion and myth cannot be laid bare by the analytic power of the intellect. Allegory reveals more than analysis, imagery more than literal description.

In ancient and tribal cultures, the soul's special teachings were passed down by word of mouth from one generation to the next. The traditional literature often has many levels of meaning, reflected by complex accretions of commentary. In Europe, alchemy is usually defined as the transmutation of base metals into gold; but at a deeper level, and for the initiate, it describes the journey of the soul, the transmutation of the raw material of the psyche into the shining and incorruptible gold of spiritual fulfilment. In the East, Tantra is superficially represented by the fierce, dark forms of deities stamping on corpses; but its inner impulse is toward the same transmutation of crude emotions into the exhilarating energies of the enlightened mind. Symbols such as these are meaningful to us as we search for ways to experience and comprehend the truths that elude literal description.

In exploring the lexicon of the soul, we inevitably encounter complications when we consider the relationship of the soul to the body. In the West, this relationship is most often perceived as an absolute dualism, but traditions which view the mind and body more holistically – for example, those which inform alternative healing, yoga, meditation – offer a different perspective. In the East, the body has never been seen as distinct from the soul. The "psychosomatic" or "subtle" body contains a network of energy channels which move spiritual energy around a complex internal network. The view that the body is inferior to the soul has been prevalent in the West – denial of the pleasures of the

EMBLEMS OF CHRISTIANITY
This figure, from a devotional commentary of the 12th century, depicts the complex network of spiritual symbols underpinning Christian beliefs.

Introduction

11

BRAHMA ON THE *HAMSA*
The great Hindu creator god, Brahma, is often depicted on his mount, the wild goose or swan (*hamsa*). The *hamsa*'s flight symbolizes the soul's yearning for release from this life.

flesh allowed the soul to escape contamination and free itself from the shackles of material existence. Similarly, in Buddhist belief, attachment to the world is the source of suffering. In striving toward self-understanding, we must engage with these ideas in ways that are meaningful to us. Do our emotions have a spiritual dimension, or can they undermine the spirit? How can we live spiritually with our bodily appetites?

An individual soul or spirit exists beyond the confines of ordinary time and space. Far from being personal, the soul may participate in the soul of the world itself, the *anima mundi*. Every natural presence in the world is perceived to have consciousness. When we recognize that the world is "ensouled", our relationship with our environment is transformed into respect and appreciation for a shared life. Conversely, when the world is seen as separate from the

Introduction

individual self, feelings of disillusion set in – a spiritual listlessness known to tribal peoples as a "loss of soul" and familiar in technological societies as *ennui*.

Yet through the various manifestations of faith – vision, symbol, ritual, discipline – we may still grasp the archetypal reality that underlies all experience. Through prayer and meditation we can see the wholeness of being and accept the interdependence of pain and pleasure as the very essence of the human condition.

MUSTANG
EFFIGIES
These effigies, hung above the main entrance to a house in Nepal, are intended to ward off evil spirits, which are believed to be ever-present.

SOUL AND COSMOS

Humankind's relationship with the Earth and the wider universe is one of its most important preoccupations. For thousands of years, belief systems have influenced people's perception of the world around them and informed their awareness and demarcation of time. The oldest religions worshipped the Earth as an all-powerful goddess, the provider of food and shelter who gave birth to all living things and reabsorbed them again after death. Many ancient communities developed sacred seasonal rituals in response to the astronomical movements that they saw in the heavens. Our diverse modern faiths seek to challenge the limitations of a materialistic, secular perspective. They emphasize the soul's place within an orchestrated cosmos, in which spiritual health is essential to personal and universal harmony.

COSMIC MAN
In the Middle
Ages each zodiac
sign was associ-
ated with a part
of the body,
re-affirming cor-
respondences
between the
individual and
an animate
universe.

THE WORLD SOUL

Many of us today feel disconnected from the natural world. We are no longer dependent upon the pattern of climate and seasons, and have largely abandoned the rituals that once expressed our intimate relationship with the Earth. Yet from the earliest times people have sensed a vital, spiritual force linking the whole of the material universe. They believed that the Earth was a living creature, animated by a soul similar to that of a human being's. In respecting the sacredness of our Earth, we acknowledge its connection with the harmony of the individual soul.

This perceived correspondence between the human and natural worlds was once underlined by the elements. Spirituality was manifested through veneration for the Earth. Many cultures continue to perceive the sacred in everything around them – all natural phenomena, from stones to mountains, trees and rivers, are thought to possess a soul, as are all animals. Through traditional rituals, some societies still attempt to influence the soul of the Earth by prayer, sacrifice and offerings, or by the working of sympathetic magic.

The ancient Greeks' fascination with the world soul was to have a profound influence on Western thought. In the *Timaeus*, Plato used a complex cosmological myth to explain the existence of the world soul. The maker-god created the universe in the form of a rotating sphere. This sphere, made of soul-matter, was produced by the harmonious fusion of earth, water, fire and air. After the creation of the universe, the remnants of

The World Soul

soul-stuff were formed into human souls. Translated into Latin, the concept of *anima mundi* re-emerged centuries later to inspire neo-Platonist philosophers, alchemists and astrologers. Human beings' spiritual purpose was thought to lie in rediscovering the universe of ideas in which the individual soul originated.

In the 20th century, the psychologist Carl Jung revealed the role that he believed connections between the soul and the cosmos still played in the unconscious. He interpreted spiritual growth as a process that allowed the creative principle animating the universe to become conscious of itself through the human mind – usually through symbols in dreams.

Scientific materialism may perceive the world as an inanimate lump of matter. Yet correspondences between the human soul and the natural world still inform our deeper consciousness through dreams, myths and the symbols of religions that bring us spiritual focus.

KRISHNA IN COSMIC FORM
This Rajasthani painting of 1890 depicts Krishna, the eighth avatar (incarnation) of the Hindu god Vishnu. Krishna revealed to his foster mother, Yashoda, that he and the world were one and the same.

The World Soul

THE GREAT MOTHER

When we are children, we rely upon our mother for nourishment and protection. Religions have often venerated the mother–child bond, and our distant ancestors sensed themselves to be children of a maternal Earth, who nourished and sheltered them.

The surface of the Earth itself was thought to be the body of a great and powerful mother, from whose regenerative womb all plant and animal life emerged and into whose arms it was returned in death. The ancient Greeks believed that the folds and undulations of the Earth represented the body of the goddess Gaia. Violation of the environment is still considered a crime in many beliefs, as shown in this description of a Native American's relationship with the Earth, written less than a hundred years ago: "You ask me to plough the ground? Shall I take a knife and tear my mother's bosom? Then when I die she will not take me to her bosom to rest."

At certain sacred locations, the landscape was especially revered, particularly

THE MATERNAL GODDESSES ASHERAH AND GAIA
This detail from the portals of San Zeno Cathedral, Verona, depicts the Canaan Asherah and the Greek Gaia suckling their children.

The Great Mother

where it evoked the female body. Living temples were created from large areas of the natural terrain, and Neolithic peoples worshipped the Earth goddess in great seasonal festivals.

The power of maternal Earth goddesses derived from their links with both

creative and destructive processes. The ambivalent role of these goddesses – bringers of birth and death, fertility and degeneration – found expression in many cultures as a polarization of imagery. The ancient Indian mother goddess, for example, survives in the Hindu pantheon as the avenging deities Kali and Durga, while her nurturing

MOTHER EARTH
This 11th-century illustration depicts Earth as a woman and emphasizes the goddess's role as mother to all living things.

qualities appear in the gentle Parvati. The Celtic goddess Epona combined the roles of warrior, healer, guardian of the dead and source of fertility.

The concept of the Earth as a goddess rendered sacred its natural curves and crevices – caves, rock clefts and springs. These were the points at which the body of the goddess opened and through which spiritual connections might be renewed. Several Earth goddesses are linked to the chthonic powers of the underworld, a connection shown by their mastery over snakes and other subterranean creatures. In Attica, initiation rituals into the Eleusinian Mysteries of Demeter enacted a symbolic descent and return of the soul to the underworld.

Aspects of devotion to an Earth goddess still appear in our beliefs today. Many modern environmental concerns display a re-emerging awareness of our profound connection with the Earth, and of the importance of responsible guardianship for our own spiritual wellbeing.

The Great Mother

THE WORLD AXIS

THE CENTRE OF THE UNIVERSE

The cosmos's sacred axis rein-forces the link between human and heavenly realms. This 16th-century Turkish chart shows the Sun at the heart of the universe.

We have always needed to feel our-selves part of a unified, ordered cosmos, whether it is described in scientific or spiritual terms. Aspiring beyond our lim-ited earthly perspective, we imagine dis-tinct but related planes of existence that bring together the gods, our living selves and the souls of the dead. Any sense of isolation from divine powers or revered ancestors has been dispelled in various cultures through the notion of the cosmic axis – a vertical col-umn, like the spinal cord, that joins the separate levels of the universe into a single entity.

This sacred axis provides a central point of time and space, from which all of creation is believed to have arisen. Such a symbolic place, which may be called the Navel of the World, the Sacred Cen-tre, the World Tree or the Cosmic Moun-tain, frequently represents a point where the gods (or their messengers) revealed themselves to humanity. For example, Mecca, where the Ka'bah, a holy Black Stone, fell from the sky and where God appeared to Ibrahim (Abraham), is the birthplace of the Prophet Muhammad and the central focus for Islamic prayer.

The Dome of the Rock in Jerusalem is another example of a world axis in an actual geographic location. The present-day Islamic shrine is built on the site of the ancient Jewish Temple of Solomon, described in a rabbinical text as the centre of the world. The foundation stone of the Temple – and of the Jewish world – set at the heart of the Muslim shrine marked the navel of a spiritual universe.

The central axis is often believed to be an aid to visionary experience – a focus enabling the soul to reconnect with a greater reality. Aboriginal peoples in Australia believed that when Numbakula, the divine being, created the ancestors in mythical time, he also made a Sky Pole from the trunk of a gum tree.

The World Axis

This pole came to represent the centre of the tribe's world. They took the pole with them wherever they travelled, to retain a link with their creator through the cosmic axis. Should the pole break, the clan would face spiritual disorientation, illness or even death.

The World Tree is a universal symbol uniting the spatial realms of experience: the heavens, the surface world and the underworld. Gods and human beings maintain their connection with each other through the three diverse realms. Ascents into the sky are a key feature of shamanism; the journey often involves a symbolic ascent of the World Tree to bring back guidance and predictions from the spirit realm.

To the Native American Navaho, the sacred corn plant represents the world axis, emerging each spring from the underworld and growing toward the sky.

THE JESSE TREE
This tree represents the divine lineage of the Hebrew king David as an axis through time.

THE WORLD TREE
In Norse myth the layers of the cosmos were united by the World Ash (right), named Yggdrasil.

CYCLES OF TIME

DAY OF
THE DEAD
The Mexican Day
of the Dead
celebrates the
idea of rebirth,
symbolized by
the flowers and
animals entwined
around this life-
size skeleton.

The passage of time arouses many complex issues in our lives. As we age, we become increasingly aware of our own mortality. This personal experience is set against other, conflicting perceptions of time – a modern, secular vision of limitless progress, in which humankind becomes increasingly sophisticated and skilled – and the very different perspectives of most spiritual beliefs. In contemplating timescales far beyond our own lifespan, we often draw upon these beliefs to point up what is significant in the day-to-day pattern of our lives.

Three of the modern world's major religions – Judaism, Islam and Christianity – place emphasis upon a finite, linear vision of time, beginning with the creation and ending in an apocalypse, after which only spiritual realms will endure. Other belief systems, notably

Hinduism, Buddhism and Jainism, draw upon a cyclical view of time in which the cosmos continually renews itself. As the "Wheel of Time" revolves through eternity, worlds are born and die; at the completion of each cycle, or *yuga*, the whole world is destroyed, only to be born again. One of the most celebrated Hindu images is Shiva in the role of Nataraja, Lord of the Dance. The god's cosmic dance represents the cycle of destruction and regeneration in the universe, symbolized by the surrounding circle of flames.

In Hinduism, the cosmic cycle is interlinked with the concept of *samsara*, in which the human soul reincarnates repeatedly. The ultimate goal is to achieve a state of spiritual perfection that enables the soul to escape from all worldly ties.

SHIVA NATARAJA
The image of Shiva as Lord of the Dance reminds Hindus of the unending process of creation and destruction.

Cycles of Time

Cycles of Time

The origin of the cosmic cycle itself is surrounded by many different myths. One tells of the creator god, Brahma, emerging from Vishnu's navel and beginning to emit the matter of the universe. Every day of Brahma's life – which lasts the equivalent of 8,640 million human years – the god's eyes open and close 1,000 times; each time they open a universe appears and each time they close it vanishes again. Each universe moves through four ages, from the Golden Age to our own age, in which suffering is all-pervasive.

The Jains depict the cosmic round as a wheel whose sections represent the ages of the world. Six ascending sections move from darkness to light and six descending ones from a noble age into a degenerate one. Jains believe that the cycle will continue for all eternity.

In ancient Egypt, the actions of the powerful creator god were interwoven with the daily course of the Sun through the heavens. The Sun god Ra, born from

the sky goddess at dawn, declined into old age in the evening. Each night the god travelled in a barque across the underworld, where he did battle with the serpent Apep to ensure rebirth the next day. In a universe both perpetually renewed and permanently imperilled, symbols of regeneration, such as the scarab beetle, assumed talismanic importance. The solar cycle became a daily exemplar of miraculous rebirth, which enabled Ra to bring light to his people.

RA IN THE UNDERWORLD
This image from an Egyptian Book of the Dead dates from *c.*1400BCE. It depicts the Sun god Ra making his nightly journey through the underworld before being triumphantly reborn the next morning.

SACRED CALENDARS

We are often aware of the apparently chaotic pace of our lives, in which artificial demarcations of time have replaced the natural patterns of the seasons and of night and day. Great seasonal festivals were central to all ancient cultures. Even today, our religious festivals retain underlying associations with the year's cycle. Increasingly shielded from the elements, we need these rituals to sustain our spiritual focus and an understanding of our role in the natural world.

Everywhere across the globe, spring festivals are primarily joyous occasions. This was traditionally a time when temples and homes were ritually cleansed and the demons of the old year expelled. Several of the customs in modern religious festivals are pagan in origin: Christian spiritual regeneration at Easter, for example, is linked with the egg, a potent symbol of rebirth, resurrection and fertility. In Teutonic myth, the egg was laid

Sacred Calendars

A CHRISTIAN
BOOK OF
HOURS
Books of Hours,
such as the
*Forester Book
of Hours* below,
guided their
readers through
the prescribed
devotions of the
Christian year.

by the Easter Hare, whose origins may be found in the sacrificial animal dedicated to Eostre (the goddess of spring, from whom Easter derived its name). The Hindu festival of Holi, which originally celebrated the growing crops, is one of India's most popular festivals – streets come alive with riotous colour.

Midsummer was often a time for fire festivals. At the summer solstice, bonfires invoked sympathetic magic to encourage the Sun to hold on to its power. Wheels of fire were sometimes sent hurtling down mountain sides, or shot into the air from high places.

Autumn is a time to celebrate the completion of the year's work: the first fruits of the harvest were offered to deities or spirits or to the souls of ancestors before feasting could

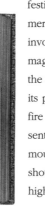

begin. Plants were often believed to have souls, which required propitiation when the crop was first cut. In ancient times, autumn festivals celebrated the dying gods of vegetation, such as the Egyptian Osiris and the Babylonian Tammuz (see page 126).

Light is a particular feature of ceremonies conducted in winter. Almost universally, light represents the power of new or enduring life, offering protection against the forces of darkness. The Jewish festival of Hanukkah commemorates the historic re-dedication of the Temple in Jerusalem when the consecrated oil used to light the candles miraculously lasted eight days. This event is celebrated each year in the ritual lighting of the Menorah, the sacred candlestick.

Seasonal festivals are still times when people turn aside from personal concerns and unite, transcending their feelings of powerlessness and the fear of elemental forces.

DIVALI
Hindus celebrate Divali on the new moon that ends the month of Ashvina (late October to early November). Lamps are lit and the goddess Lakshmi is invited into the home to bring the family luck in the coming year.

SACRED SKIES

Since earliest times, people have believed the star-studded vault of night to represent the entrance to another cosmic realm – sometimes the resting-place of our souls, often thought to fly upward from the body after death; sometimes the home of the gods who govern human existence. As we gather more scientific data about the stars and planets of our galaxy, we realize how much still eludes us in trying to comprehend the cosmos in which we live.

The first communities, observing the movements of the Sun and Moon, were aware that the relationship between Earth and sky affected every part of their existence. Rituals celebrated the year's changing seasons and reinforced sacred links between the heavens and the Earth. Even today, the dates of many holy festivals, such as Passover, Easter, Holi and the Islamic fasting month of Ramadan, are all determined by an

Sacred Skies

ancient lunar calendar, and each may fall upon different dates annually.

Early people's astonishingly accurate knowledge of celestial patterns is demonstrated by the precise alignment of Neolithic stone structures, such as Stonehenge in southern England, with the positions of the Sun and Moon at key moments in the year. The Babylonians divided the sky into 36 sections and later identified 12 constellations, which subsequently formed the basis of the Greek zodiac, along the ecliptic (the Sun's apparent path around the Earth). This ecliptic-based system remains central to Western astrology and astronomy. The Maya city of Chichén Itzá, built *c.*600–830CE, contains an elaborate observatory orientated toward several astronomical events.

Every culture has attached sacred importance to the most conspicuous

A CREE IMAGE OF THE MOON
Most cultures view the Moon as female, but hunting societies – such as the Native American Cree, who often trap animals at night – may see the Moon as a male deity.

bodies in the sky, the Sun and Moon. The Moon often came to be perceived as female and the Sun as male – the divine father or eye of the world. The Moon, with its phases of dark and light, symbolizes the rhythm of cosmic cycles and of death and rebirth.

To early peoples, the movements of Sun, Moon and planets against the stars were symbolic of heavenly order and harmony, to which the individual soul was profoundly linked. For millennia, no wars were fought, treaties signed, or marriages arranged, until the heavens were scanned for good or bad omens. Weather conditions were also thought to reflect the state of harmony on Earth. In China, the Emperor's right to rule was called into question by evil omens in the sky.

THE ASCENT OF ELIJAH
Great biblical events are often heralded by unusual weather. This Russian icon (below) depicts a whirlwind propelling the prophet Elijah upward in a chariot of fire.

THE WORLD OF ILLUSION

PLATO'S CAVE OF SHADOWS

Plato taught that we should be open to the possibility of higher realities, rather than relying on our five senses for information.

As human beings, we all share a need to understand our soul's relationship with the universe, and to see beyond the limitations and confusions of our individual lives. In modern, secular cultures, spiritual meanings may become diminished or obscured by the pressures to achieve material success. We may feel that we now inhabit an "unreal" world, in which science and commerce have distorted an ancient awareness of our true place in the cosmos.

Ancient Greek philosophers were the first to link the nature of the soul with a radical exploration of illusion and reality. In Plato's highly influential writings, true reality was perceived to lie in the realm of "ideas" or "forms" that can be

understood by our reason – rather than in the world of the senses, where nothing is permanent. This realm of ideas informs all sensual experience: a black dog, for example, derives its form from the universal idea of a dog and the universal idea of blackness. The human soul, Plato wrote, yearns to return to its true origins in this realm, and to escape from the constraints of a physical body.

To illustrate his theory, Plato described an underground cave in which chained prisoners faced the rear wall, on which they saw a variety of dancing shadows. The prisoners, who had never seen any other reality, imagined that the shadows were the real world.

Is the world as it seems to be? Is there any way to see beyond the reality presented through our senses? Such profound questions have dominated

A BUTTERFLY DREAM
The *Book of Zhuang Zi*, written by Zhuang Zhou in the 3rd century BCE, uses the philosophical questions posed by a dream to encourage readers to reassess their true identities (see page 40).

The World of Illusion

The World of Illusion

the traditions of philosophy and spirituality in both East and West. A story by the Daoist philosopher Zhuang Zhou shows how bewildering the soul's search for true identity can be. The story describes how Zhuang Zhou awakes after dreaming that he was a butterfly: " ... although he was awake he did not know if he was Zhuang Zhou dreaming that he was a butterfly, or a butterfly dreaming that he was Zhuang Zhou."

Whereas the philosopher tries to pin down reality through conceptual thought, spiritual traditions look for ways of experiencing it directly. In Daoism, the ideal is *wu wei*, non-doing or non-action, which is not intent upon any result. If the individual soul is in harmony with reality, the mind can return to original clarity, stillness, tranquillity, silence. The flickering shadows of sense perceptions may then be seen against the backdrop of this immense and absolute stillness.

A DAOIST
MONK
MEDITATING
Daoist meditation aims to empty the mind of thoughts that are distorted by an individual's consciousness. This 13th-century Chinese woodblock features Sima Chengzhen, an 8th-century Daoist master.

ILLUSION AND EGO

Those who follow spiritual beliefs do not view philosophical enquiry as an end in itself: it is simply one of many ways to help us recognize that the satisfaction of appetites may not be the only valid focus of our existence. In many religions this is accompanied by the acknowledgment that preoccupation with our individual selves is part of the complex of illusions that we must discard.

Freedom from the demands of the ego is the primary spiritual goal of most Eastern religions, and the means by which release from the unending cycle of rebirth (see page 29), may be found. In Hinduism, every action binds an individual soul more closely to the world of illusion or enables it to move nearer to an ideal of virtuous, disinterested detachment. The Jain religion similarly seeks a withdrawal from the world through disciplines of mental and physical austerity, while an essential tenet of Buddhism is the premise of enlightenment through negation of egotism.

The progress toward such spiritual liberation is exemplified by the Buddha's own life. Born Prince Siddhartha in northern India, as a young man he became consumed by the desire to find meaning in the trials of human existence. After years as a wandering ascetic, Siddhartha eventually came to rest under what is known as the Bodhi Tree. There he perceived that false adherence to the ego prompted a terrible chain reaction: in trying to defend an illusory sense of self, people continued to be ignorant of their true nature and were destined to suffer again and again. He recognized that his own mind had been clinging to insubstantial projections. When Siddhartha had this realization, he touched the ground and called the Earth to witness his spiritual release from the illusory world of *samsara*, the endless cycle of rebirth. At that moment he became Buddha, the awakened one.

The insights that the Buddha gained at the Bodhi Tree became the essence of his teaching on the Four Noble Truths. In common with other religions of the East, as well as some Western mystical traditions, the Buddha believed that attempts to capture spiritual truth in written form were bound to fail. Ultimate reality could only be grasped through the power of symbol. Words merely offered pointers toward truth. At one of his most famous sermons, in front of thousands of people, the Buddha sat in silence and simply held up a flower.

THE
BODHI TREE
The famous
tree (left) under
which the Bud-
dha gained
enlightenment.

MARA'S ARMIES
Armies sent by
Mara, the demon,
tried in vain to
oust Siddhartha
from beneath the
Bodhi Tree.

PANTHEONS OF THE GODS

THE GREEK PANTHEON
This ancient Greek relief shows the supreme god Zeus with three of his children: Athene, Apollo and Artemis.

For many of us, the life of the soul is linked with our chosen religion. We look to sacred texts and rituals for a better understanding of the essential truths that both inform and transcend our world. Patterns of worship vary widely between different belief systems, as do the manifestations that divine power assumes. Yet all faiths share a common purpose: to open our eyes to the reality of the divine.

Most of the world's great religions divide into monotheistic and pantheistic systems of belief. Some focus upon the existence of a single divine power; others are structured around one supreme being with many different aspects; yet others encompass the worship of a large number of gods and goddesses.

The Hindu religion has evolved a highly complex pantheon. Its multiplicity of gods and goddesses are manifestations of the supreme power of *brahman* – a pure consciousness whose authority pervades and dominates the cosmos. Yet individual Hindu gods are worshipped in an extraordinarily wide variety of forms. Shiva, for example, is simultaneously revered as the Lord of the Dance who represents and controls the harmonious movements of the universe (see page 29); as the naked god of

Pantheons of the Gods

Pantheons of the Gods

asceticism; and as the creative force of male sexual energy (see pages 79–80).

The gods and goddesses of early religions tend to have been recognized as individual powers, each retaining their own sphere of influence. They were often linked to the forces of the elements and the seasons. Largely indifferent to

THE KAʿBAH
This detail from a 9th-century Koran shows the Kaʿbah. Housed within the Great Mosque at Mecca the Kaʿbah is Islam's holiest shrine, used for the exclusive worship of Allah.

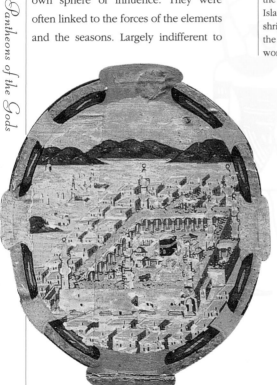

human suffering, these divinities were worshipped for their power. The sophisticated religions of the ancient Greeks and Romans also featured deities whose intervention lacked a consistent moral imperative. Instead, they epitomized contradictory features of the human psyche: sexual love, jealousy, delight in war, serenity and wisdom, trickery and lust.

The three major Western religions – Judaism, Christianity and Islam – affirm the same fundamental doctrine that there is only one, omnipotent God. These monotheistic religions perceive time and history as linear and finite, and share the conviction that God made himself known to his chosen followers through a form of special revelation. All three religions have the same root texts and the same ancient mythology, and acknowledge the holiness of Jerusalem. They also believe in a divine antithesis: a powerful spirit of evil, personified by Satan, the fallen angel of light.

Pantheons of the Gods

BALANCING HEAVEN AND EARTH

IKEBANA
Shinto, the
native Japanese
religion, teaches
a reverence for
all natural things.
This philosophy
was adopted by
practitioners of
ikebana, who
arrange flowers
as a means of
expressing their
spiritual ideals.

Many of us experience deep spiritual feelings in a natural environment. In tending our gardens or admiring the countryside, we recognize and celebrate the sacredness of our physical world. Nature's abundance reveals a harmonious balance of Earth and the heavens that nourishes the individual soul.

The indigenous religion of Japan is Shinto – the so-called "Way of the *kami*", or gods. A pantheistic religion, Shinto recognizes a multiplicity of deities produced from the primal union of a divine brother and sister, Izanagi and Izanami. *Kami* are essentially divine spirits who enter the world and imbue it with sacred life. The *kami*'s presence is closely associated with the rituals and activities of daily existence. This extends in one instance to divine parentage – the

Japanese imperial family traces its descent from the powerful Sun goddess Amaterasu, although the Emperor no longer claims to be a living god.

Kami are essentially guardian spirits of the land, linked to the elements, natural features and agriculture. The rice goddess, for example, is petitioned annually for assistance with the growing and harvesting of her crop.

Shrines and temples become extremely important in a localized religion without traditional scriptures or rigid doctrines. Shinto worshippers prefer simple shrines located at sacred sites. The shrines, placed amid trees and gardens, and containing pure water in stone troughs, underscore the relation of human beings to the natural world.

Yet *kami* are not solely nature spirits, a fact that has enabled Shinto to retain its influence in a modern, industrialized Japan. They are associated with the arts, leisure activities and even manufacturing. *Kami* maintain a domestic presence

Balancing Heaven and Earth

too. A "god shelf" in the home supports daily offerings of salt, rice and water, inviting the divine spirit to participate in, and bring harmony to, the rituals that characterize everyday family life.

Shinto is very much a personal religion, which finds communal expression in *matsuri* – regional festivals in honour of the *kami*. Such ceremonies are joyous, reflecting Shinto's vitality and relevance as a "life religion" that links spirituality with the physical world.

THE SHINTO
GATEWAY TO
THE GODS
To enter a
Japanese Shinto
shrine, a worshipper must
first pass under
the *torii*. This
ceremonial gate
represents the
threshold separating the secular
world from the
sacred world of
the *kami* (gods).

DIVINATION

DIVINATION
PLATE
Many practices
of divination
involve throwing
objects upon a
chart and inter-
preting the
pattern that is
formed when
they fall. In
Nigeria, diviners
make predictions
from the shapes
made by rice
or seeds on
special plates.

All of us have wished, on occasion, to be able to predict the future and discover the significance of patterns of incident, such as recurring encounters or dreams, that we may recognize in our lives. Divination uses a symbolic key to decipher the underlying meaning of physical forms. Knowledge of the future and manifestations of divine will have been sought in many strange guises, including the entrails of sacrificed animals, configurations of smoke from burning incense, and cloud formations. The principle behind divination, known as synchronicity, recognizes an essential link between inner and outer reality. We are not isolated beings but part of a unified

Divination

cosmos, and great wisdom can be found through analyzing the apparently random phenomena of the physical world.

The ancient Chinese *Yi Jing* ("The Book of Changes") is the world's oldest surviving complete divinatory system. Its core text dates from well before 1500 BCE and contains the roots of both Daoism and Confucianism. The *Yi Jing* uses yarrow sticks to compose up to 64 hexagons. The dynamic interaction between complementary pairs of opposites is believed to create images that mirror the structure of the human psyche.

Shamanic divinatory practices centre on direct encounter with the spirit world. The shaman of the Native American Ojibway people invokes his or her personal guardian spirits, or *pawagonak*. Strange songs uttered by the spirit voices signal the start of the divination process.

Oracles have been an important feature of divination in the early civilizations of both East and West. Highly respected and often sacred mediators engaged in dialogue with the gods, sometimes through utterances and movements produced in an ecstatic trance. In taking counsel from an oracle, an individual sought to act in harmony with the governing principles of both the physical and spiritual worlds.

The Tibetans practise many forms of divination. Before Chinese control was established, the State Oracle was a paid government official whose national duty involved entering into trance states to talk with the gods.

Scientific materialism, often dismissive of divination, has still to resolve the vast complexities of cause and effect. Science may yet come to support the ancient belief that our universe possesses a complex, intelligent structure, upon which the human psyche ultimately depends.

TAROT CARDS
One of the best-known forms of divination in the West uses Tarot cards. The cards' symbols form a pattern of past, present and future feelings and events which are interpreted by the diviner.

Divination

Sacred Space

SACRED SPACE

In visiting sacred places we often experience a distinct spiritual charge. The divine presence that we sense in such places is often reinforced by architecture and decoration that reflect our aspirations toward the heavens.

A sacred place requires a clear spiritual focus and separation from its physical surroundings. The word "temple" originates from the Latin *templum*, meaning a piece of land marked off from ordinary uses and dedicated to a god. The architecture of sacred buildings must attempt to capture the divine presence and reveal it to the worshipper, together with the recognition that a transcendent deity is infinitely greater than any physical site. The dome of an Islamic mosque or a Christian

STUPAS
*Stupa*s are dome-shaped monuments that are believed to house the bodily relics of the Buddha and his prominent disciples. Their sacred architecture is thought to represent the Buddha's path to liberation.

TEMPLE OF AMUN
The vast Egyptian temple at Karnak is dedicated to Amun, the creator god. The temple's pillars are carved with papyrus flowers, evoking the Egyptian creation myth of a primordial island that remained after the flood waters had finally receded.

cathedral directs the worshipper's gaze toward the heavens and the inexpressible majesty of God. Many Christian Orthodox churches feature the Byzantine interpretation of Christ Pantocrator – Ruler of All Things – (see page 219) inside the central dome or the apse. The curve of the dome surrounds the viewer with the awe and immediacy of divine encounter.

Neither synagogues nor mosques contain any representations of the deity; divine authority is revealed instead through the venerated word. The Ark containing the holy scrolls of the Jewish Torah is the focus of all synagogue rituals, and is always set into the wall facing the Temple Mount in Jerusalem. In Islam, the perfection of Allah is manifested through the elaborate inscriptions from the Koran on the walls of the mosque. The intricate patterning of mosaics is both harmonious and mesmerizing, charged with spiritual meaning. As the dome spreads outward, geometric patterns represent the inter-

Sacred Space

THE TEMPLE OF HEAVEN Reflecting Confucian belief, this ceiling in the Temple of Heaven, Beijing, reproduces the geometric structure of heaven.

woven ordering of Creation around a central, omnipotent God.

In contrast, Hindu temples provide a more literal dwelling-place for the individual deity, who is believed to reside within the sculpted image usually located in the innermost sanctuary. Worship is manifested through daily rituals of waking, dressing, bathing and feeding this image. A classic Hindu temple includes a rising tower above the inner sanctuary, symbolizing Mount Meru, the axis (see page 24) of the spiritual universe. The ground plan, in the form of a *mandala*, represents both a map of the cosmos and the soul's progress through meditation toward enlightenment.

Different cultures have always sought to live close to their gods, and to reinforce links between physical and spiritual worlds. The spire of a cathedral, the minaret of a mosque and the Buddhist *stupa* all emphasize the subordination of earthly existence to the life of the soul.

Sacred Space

CELESTIAL REALMS

AMATERASU
The Sun goddess Amaterasu has ruled the Shinto pantheon since vanquishing her brother Susano. Her retreat into a cave brought the world darkness and misery until she re-emerged.

The beauty and magnitude of the heavens have fascinated us from the earliest times. Studded with stars, planets, the Sun and the Moon, the immense revolving vault of sky symbolizes the soul's transcendence of the material world. Many systems of belief have interpreted the movement of heavenly bodies as the divine actions of gods and goddesses.

Celestial Realms

THE
GREAT BEAR
This Chinese
image shows
the Great Bear
constellation,
representing the
energy that creat-
ed the universe.

COMETS
Comets, with
their stream-
ing fiery tails,
were often
thought to be
expressions of
divine wrath,
particularly of
the Sun gods.

A Chart of the Heavens

An Indian astrological chart of the 19th century, featuring the signs of the Eastern zodiac. Ancient Vedic texts interpreted movements of the "heavenly bodies", or *jyotis*, determining the most auspicious time to conduct religious sacrifices.

The Chariot of the Sun

The Temple of the Sun at Konarak in India was built in honour of Surya, the Sun god, in the 13th century. Its structure represents the chariot he drove across the heavens.

GODS

Jews, Christians and Muslims worship one God as the creator and ruler of the universe. In pantheistic accounts there is often a supreme deity, who achieved his position by force of arms or through having created the other gods. In some myths, the supreme god is an abstract force who withdrew after creating the universe. In contrast, gods of nature are tangible presences, manifest in the landscape and elements.

ODIN
The Norse god Odin carried the spear of Tiwaz, which gave him control of battles. He sacrificed an eye to obtain knowledge.

THE JUDEO-CHRISTIAN GOD

In Genesis, God has human attributes, such as walking and talk-ing. This painting of the Garden of Eden, dating from the late 15th century, shows him as a wise old man.

Gods

SUSANO
Embodying disorder, the Shinto storm god Susano was expelled from heaven for trying to depose his sister, the Sun goddess.

AMUN-RA
Egypt's greatest god, Amun-Ra was a combination of Amun and the Sun god Ra. He was usually shown as a man crowned with two tall plumes.

KRISHNA
The Hindu god Krishna righted many wrongs and brought joy and love into the world. An 18th-century painting.

GODDESSES

Goddesses

SELQET
This statue from
the tomb of
Tutankhamun is
of Selqet, the
Egyptian scorpion
goddess. As the
wife of the Sun
god, Ra, she was
a fertility god-
dess, presiding
over childbirth
and the family.

Our earliest ancestors viewed childbirth
as a magical process. Linking the fertility
of women with the fertility of the Earth,
they worshipped a supreme deity, the
Great Goddess, who gave, maintained
and finally took back life. As humans
changed from a migratory existence to a
more stationary lifestyle, their societies
became increasingly patriarchal and the
status of the Goddess was gradually
eroded. First she had a son or took a
lover; then she was worshipped as
the equal partner of a god; finally, she
was seen as the wife, mother, sister
or daughter of a supreme god, or
was demonized as a witch or
monster. Today, echoes of
the Great Goddess can be
found worldwide. In China, Kwan-Yin
is the generous and compassionate
mother; the Hindu Durga is an avenger
of wrongs; and the Christian Virgin
Mary is the spotless Queen of Heaven.

Goddesses

KWAN-YIN
The Chinese goddess of mercy (above) is important to women and children.

DEMETER
The Greek fertility goddess (below) governed the Earth's productivity.

Goddesses

THE VIRGIN MARY

In the New Testament, Mary is a virgin when she is told that she will be the mother of Jesus.

DURGA
Durga (left) is the
warrior aspect of
the great Hindu
goddess Devi.
The tiger Durga
rides symbolizes
her great power.

APHRODITE
This bronze head
(above) of
Aphrodite – the
Greek goddess of
love renowned
for her beauty –
dates from
the 2nd or 1st
century BCE.

BODY
AND SOUL

chapter two

The contrast between the finite existence of our physical bodies and the enduring life of the soul lies at the heart of many spiritual beliefs. We are subject to the inexorable processes of ageing and death, but faith in the soul's afterlife acknowledges these as the prelude to a greater reality. The demands of our bodies, especially for sensual pleasures, are often considered antithetical to the spiritual path. However, some religious traditions consider our bodies to be essential vehicles of divine worship. Through the ecstatic sexual union of Tantric belief, or the sacred actions of supplication, dance, pilgrimage and sacrifice, devotees transcend the physical to approach and celebrate the spiritual.

THE SOUL IN THE BODY

PAIN AND RITUAL
Flagellation, depicted in this 1st-century BCE Roman mural, was part of the orgiastic rites of the Roman god Bacchus.

In recent times there has been an unprecedented obsession in the West with youth and physical beauty. This has coincided with a significant decline in religious faith and practice. Many believe that by abandoning our spiritual values and worshipping the physical, we have created a damagingly narcissistic culture. As a society we have neglected the relationship between the physical body and the needs of the soul. Yet this relationship is an important ingredient in all human systems of belief.

Early civilizations revered the regenerative power of the natural world, and the human body provided an appropriate vehicle of worship. The cycle of the seasons, and the associated rhythms of life and death, were celebrated in countless rituals. Physical actions were often re-enacted in religious ceremonies to express the achievement of a spiritual state. For example, the Celts in Cornwall, England, symbolically enacted their spiritual rebirth by climbing through a hole in a sacred stone near Morvah.

Later religious traditions often viewed the body as impure and inferior to the soul. Plato taught that the soul belonged to a constant world of ideas, to

RAJA YOGA
A practitioner of Raja Yoga, which rejects the body as an illusion.

The Soul in the Body

The Soul in the Body

which it longed to return. To achieve release, the individual should resist the body's contaminating influence, and focus upon a transcendent spiritual ideal. Otherwise, the soul could not escape from the material world and would be reborn in gross animal form.

The early Christians drew upon other faiths, including Manichaeism, for many of their views on the body. The founder of Manichaeism, Mani, preached across the Persian Empire in the 3rd century CE. He taught that matter was evil, advocating asceticism and celibacy in the search for spiritual truth. Several early Christians were converts from Manichaeism and retained some of their old beliefs; bodily urges were viewed with fear or contempt.

Despite the Church's waning influence, its revulsion for the body has remained in our subconscious. Residual insecurity about the body underlies most human experiences. Accepting the relationship of soul and body entails coming to terms with life's hardest lessons.

LILITH

Originally a Sumerian wind goddess, Lilith features in Hebrew scriptures as a demonic queen. She was later said to be the first woman, who deserted her husband Adam. Lilith's evil influence was thought to cause men to ejaculate as they slept.

MALE AND FEMALE

Male and Female

HARI-HARA

In Hindu myth, Hari-Hara is a combination of the two male gods Vishnu the Preserver (shown in blue) and Shiva the Destroyer (wearing a tiger skin).

In our struggle to make sense of ourselves and our world, we have often tried to explain or enact our feelings of isolation, separation and longing. Most of our creation myths tell how a single, total principle divided to form men and women, and many of the world's faiths contain an element of reunification, physical or spiritual, that is a relic from a much older religion. Elemental forces have often been assigned gender and their union and separation linked to the decay and regeneration of human life. Gender difference has gained spiritual importance as a symbol of polarity – the creative power that exists between all dualisms and may be harmonious and complementary or conflicting and discordant.

This concept of polarity pervading the universe was expressed in the revered Daoist classic the *Dao De Jing* by the *ying-yang* symbol (see background image). The cosmic antitheses of female and male, night and day, Earth and sky, are held in a mutually dependent synthesis. Each side of the symbol contains within itself the seed of the other, bringing movement and change through their perpetual union and maintaining the harmony of the universe.

The Sun and the Moon have been the most enduring symbols of male and female polarity. The Sun has been viewed as male by many different belief systems. In ancient Egypt, the Sun god Ra was the supreme power at the heart of the cosmos (see page 31). Male Sun gods are invested with "masculine" attributes, such as great physical strength and prowess in battle. The Aztec Sun god Huitzilopochtli, for example, was

Male and Female

Male and Female

also worshipped as the god of war, and conflict became a form of veneration for a civilization that linked its conquests to the victory of day over night.

By contrast, the Moon is often personified as female, symbolizing the rhythms of monthly change. Its cycle of appearance, growth and disappearance has been associated with the power of female Moon deities over birth, death and resurrection. Representing the dark, intuitive aspects of nature, she regulated tides, rain and the seasons. Because of the Moon's power over unpredictable forces, she was often portrayed as the controller of individual destinies.

A complementary harmony between male and female principles was the goal of Western alchemy. Symbolically the male was sulphur, depicted as red, solar, hot and active; while mercury was female – white, lunar, cold and passive. These two principles were set in conflict, to be reconciled by the skilful alchemist in the form of the Red King and White,

PHASES OF
THE MOON
Many systems of belief have related the cyclical waxing and waning of the Moon to the natural cycle of birth, growth and decay.

Queen. The philosopher's stone, the legendary key to enlightenment, was believed to derive from their union.

Such a reconciliation of opposites was often symbolized by the union of deities. Isis and Osiris, Dumuzi and Inanna, Shiva and Parvati are all examples of creative, powerful, divine partnerships. The *hieros gamos*, or sacred marriage, of the Greek god Zeus and his sister Hera was celebrated in rituals at Samos and Argos as the wedding of heaven and Earth. Polynesian mythology also features a divine marriage: Hawaiians traditionally worshipped rock formations that resembled paired male and female genitalia, believing them to symbolize the union of their ancestral gods.

The sacred marriage appears in transmuted form in Judeo-Christian belief. The biblical Song of Songs, which on the surface is a secular love poem, has been interpreted as a dialogue between either God and Israel or Jesus and the Church.

Male and Female

SEXUAL ENERGY

SHIVA *LINGA*
The *linga*
(phallus) is
worshipped by
Hindus as the
incarnate form
of the god Shiva.
It is often shown
set inside the
yoni (vulva), as
here, forming a
complementary
union of
antitheses.

The sex drive is a primary physical instinct, integral to the survival of humankind. Its power and influence over our behaviour have been recognized by every culture. Sexuality has been considered both a distraction from, and a manifestation of, spiritual life. Some faiths have seen sex as a chain linking the soul to the material world; others have perceived erotic activity to be a vehicle of transcendence, and ecstasy an expression of the highest spiritual energy.

The creation of the cosmos is often explained by divine sexual union. Ancient Egyptian myths posited that the deities Osiris, Isis, Seth and Nepthys were born from the embrace of the Sky goddess Nut with the Earth god Geb. Vedic hymns describe the exploits of Prajapati, who couples repeatedly with the dawn to create the Earth's species.

Early spiritual beliefs often included sexual activity as an aspect of worship. Erotic energies were held to be sacred in many goddess-orientated religions, such as that of the Sumerian deity Inanna, whose sexual congress with the king Dumuzi was associated with the annual regeneration of crops. Sacred prostitutes featured in the religious traditions of ancient Greece, Rome and Mesopotamia.

The paradoxical nature of the Hindu god Shiva, lord of asceticism and regeneration, is epitomized by the *linga* form in which he is worshipped. Erect yet never spilling seed, the *linga* (phallus) balances ascetic restraint with infinite

Sexual Energy

Sexual Energy

A modern print
by J. Singh Shyam
depicts Shiva's
head within the
yoni, a symbol
of the vulva.

procreative potential. The *linga* is usually
set within a *yoni*, symbolizing the vulva
and female energy. Practitioners of Hindu
Tantra may enter into ritual sexual congress to emulate the union of Shiva and
the manifestation of the Goddess, Shakti.

Western monotheistic religions have
generally regarded sexuality with suspi-
cion or ambivalence. Both Judaism and
Islam acknowledge the pleasures of sexual expression within marriage for the
purposes of procreation,
which may be inter-
spersed with periods of
ritual abstinence. In the
early Christian Church, sex
was perceived as essentially
sinful; woman assumed the
legacy of Eve as the instrument of sensual temptation.

Procreation in wedlock
became the only permissible
reason for sexual activity, and
even that was seen as inferior
to celibacy by some ascetics.

PILGRIMAGE

There are times in our lives when we may feel that a physical journey to a sacred place – as an act of devotion, penance or thanksgiving, or to fulfil a vow – will further our spiritual development. Most world religions revere certain temples, cities or natural features because they are historically linked to their gods or prophets. Sometimes, as with Jerusalem, sites are important to more than one religion, perhaps suggesting that they have a fundamental, even intrinsic, sacredness. Buddhists and Jains visit the Ganges Basin, where both the historical Buddha and Mahavira, the Jain saint, lived, taught and died. The river Ganges itself is sacred to Hindus, and millions each year cleanse themselves in its waters, hoping to wash away their sins.

Some pilgrims, believing that their prayers are more likely to be heard if offered in a holy place, will journey hundreds of miles to make a specific

PILGRIMS AT KEDARNATH
The Hindu temple at Kedarnath is situated in the Himalayas, near the source of the Ganges. The river, temple and surrounding area are important pilgrimage sites.

Pilgrimage

Pilgrimage

request. During the Middle Ages, thousands of Christians undertook pilgrimages to Jerusalem, Rome, Santiago de Compostela, Canterbury and Walsingham. Since then, other destinations, such as Lourdes in France, have gained a reputation for granting wishes or for healing.

Certain religions demand that specific pilgrimages are undertaken by their worshippers. The last of the Five Pillars of Islam, for example, states that every Muslim who is physically able should journey to Mecca in Saudi Arabia at least once in his or her lifetime. The *hajj*, as this pilgrimage is called, is believed to bestow great merit and to wash away all sins.

Upon arrival in Mecca, the pilgrim enters a state of ritual purity by bathing and putting on two simple pieces of white cloth. Women wear additional garments to cover their legs and faces. The

SCALLOP
SHELLS
Pilgrims visiting
St James's shrine
at Compostela in
Spain traditionally
wore a scallop
shell on their
clothing. Initially
linked to the
saint, the shell
eventually became
a general symbol
of Christian
pilgrimage.

pilgrim then sets out for the Great Mosque. In the centre of the mosque is the Ka'bah, a black shrine originally dedicated to pre-Islamic gods, but cleansed and re-dedicated by the Prophet Muhammad. It contains a black stone, possibly a meteorite, which some believe was found by Adam, the first man. The initial rite of the pilgrimage is the circumambulation: the devotee circles the Ka'bah seven times. The pilgrim then travels to the Plain of Arafat, where the Prophet gave his last sermon. Here, he or she stands in repentance on the Mount of Mercy, seeking release, cleansing and oneness with God.

CARAVAN TO MECCA

This illustration by Hariri, taken from a mid-13th-century Persian manuscript, portrays a company of travellers journeying to Mecca to make the *hajj*, or pilgrimage.

Pilgrimage

SACRED DANCE

Sacred Dance

When, having seen the Ark of the Covenant safely returned, the Bible records that David "danced before the Lord with all his might" (Second Book of Samuel, 6.14), he was responding to an instinct in all of us to dance for joy or thanksgiving. Through the ages, the ancient emotions that dance can stir within participants and spectators alike have been drawn upon during rituals of birth, renewal, love, death and war.

There are many different kinds of sacred dance. Some, such as the dances of the Indian temple prostitutes, or *devadasi*s, unfurl slowly using a vast vocabulary of hand gestures and facial expressions. Others are wild and uninhibited, such as the energy-summoning dances of the San (Bushmen) of the Kalahari. Dances are performed to overcome evil spirits, ensure good crops, cure sickness, meet the ancestors, defeat enemies, or to please the gods. In some

EKOI TRIBE DANCE MASK Masks conceal the identities of the performers and confer on them the attributes and power of the deity, spirit or animal that they are impersonating.

sacred dances, the performer takes on the identity of the divine being; for this to be effective, the costume must express the deity's magical quality. Masks are particularly signifi-cant because they contain the concen-trated power of the god or spirit, trans-forming the dancers into magical beings.

Dance and rhythmical music often induce changes in

Sacred Dance

consciousness: trance and ecstatic states are common (see pages 226–228). The dance of the Mevlevi Order of Ottoman Sufis, founded in the 13th century, incorporated trance. Known as the "Whirling Dervishes", they sought ecstasy through spinning around in a movement intended to represent the order of the heavenly spheres. During the dance, one hand was held in the air, open to receive the Divine Essence, and the other was held toward the ground. Thus the dancers were symbolically linked to heaven and Earth.

Many sacred dances contain elements of terrestrial and spiritual renewal. Modern European maypole and morris dances originated in ancient round dances, performed to aid the Sun's journey through the heavens. In contrast, during the four-day Native American Sun Dance participants would endure fasting and self-torture in order to assure the tribe's prosperity.

In the late 19th century, Native American dance rituals were combined

BULL LEAPING
In ancient Crete, young dancers somersaulted over a bull – a symbol of divine potency – in a form of fertility ritual.

with Christian elements in the Shaker Church. Members of the sect practised a rolling exercise, doubling the head and feet together and rolling over like a hoop. Hasidic Jews perform a circular dance, in which each participant puts his hands on the shoulders of his neighbours in a symbol of unity.

THE ACT OF PRAYER

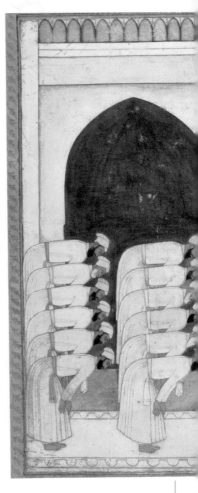

Many of us associate prayer with quiet reflection in a place removed from the distractions of everyday life. As a personal communication with or petition to the divine, prayer is understood primarily as involving the soul. In most spiritual traditions, prayer is believed to be at its most powerful when it combines reiterated physical action and speech.

ISLAMIC PRAYER
An 18th-century Mughal painting depicting the *ruku* bow at Friday prayers in a mosque.

Preparation for prayer often includes ablution. Shinto worshippers wash their hands and rinse their mouths before ringing a bell or clapping to attract the gods' attention. Participants in North American traditions are brushed with burnt sweet-grass to purify them.

The characteristic bodily attitudes of prayer – bowing, kneeling, prostration – are gestures of humble submission. On entering a church or approaching the altar, Roman Catholics touch one knee to the ground and make the sign of the Cross. When visiting a temple, Hindu worshippers prostrate themselves in prayer outside the inner sanctuary, which only priests can enter.

Most organized prayers take one of five standard forms: supplication, adoration, praise, contrition or thanksgiving. While supplicating and contrite prayers are usually offered kneeling or bowing, gods may be praised or thanked standing with arms outstretched. The latter position invites the divine to enter into the heart. Hand positions are also important. During Hindu and Buddhist rituals and dances, participants use *mudra*s, or hand gestures, to convey hundreds of different concepts or principles.

Although private prayer is recognized by every religion, public prayer as part of a congregation is thought by many traditions to be more uplifting. Jewish and Christian religious services combine song, readings and set prayers to create a specific atmosphere. Prayer is one of the Five Pillars of the Islamic faith, and on Friday afternoons obligatory congregational prayers are held at the mosque, including the *ruku*, or straight-legged bow (see picture, pages 88–89).

RITUAL HAND GESTURES
*Mudra*s, or hand gestures, are used in Hindu and Buddhist rituals and dances to convey key religious principles. A type of visual shorthand, this symbolic language uses hundreds of positions.

The Act of Prayer

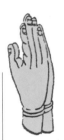   

THE WAY OF THE WARRIOR

The Way of the Warrior

ARCHANGEL MICHAEL
As the Christian champion, Michael is usually portrayed wearing the breastplate of righteousness and the shield of faith. His sword is the word of God.

To many of us, war is a great evil and has no place in a civilized society. However, warrior cultures were once widespread, and their influence can be found in the teaching and rituals of almost all of the world's religions. Great warriors developed a fearlessness in the face of danger that allowed them to directly overcome physical and spiritual obstacles.

The Hindu holy book, the *Bhagavad Gita*, tells the story of Arjuna, a leading Pandava warrior, who was fighting for control of his country against the Kauravas. When Arjuna experienced doubt about the morality of the battle he was about to enter, the god Krishna explained that it was not possible for Arjuna, as an embodied soul, to stand back from the conflict. However, what binds us to the painful wheel of rebirth is emotional attachment in action, not action itself. The higher "self" is not involved in

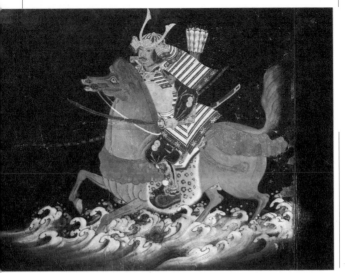

The Way of the Warrior

conflict. According to Krishna, if Arjuna did not act from personal attachment, he could perform his role on the battlefield knowing that his innermost nature would be untouched by all that took place.

Many religions teach that warfare is permissible, and even desirable, in defence of the faith. In the 11th, 12th and 13th centuries the Christian powers of Europe raised armies to retake the Holy Land from the Muslim Turks.

THE SAMURAI Members of the Japanese warrior caste were renowned for their military skills, stoicism and bravery. Contact with Buddhist priests taught them to cultivate fearlessness toward death.

Known as the Crusades, these military expeditions were infamous for their brutal treatment of the enemy. The unofficial Sixth Pillar of Islam is *jihad*, or striving, which is usually taken to mean holy war against the infidels. In the face of Mughal hostility, the tenth Sikh Guru, Gobind Singh, instigated the Rahit, a code of discipline which obliges all Sikhs to carry a sword or dagger.

In medieval Japan, contact between the samurai warrior class and Buddhist priests gave rise to new ideas about warriorship. Students of the martial arts learned to counter force without the use of aggression. Their aim was self-knowledge, leading to spiritual realization, and the weapons that had been used for slaughter were transformed into powerful spiritual tools.

Today, most of us acknowledge our wariness of aggressive physical energy, but the conquering hero who subdues evil remains an essential component of the human psyche. .

SACRIFICE

Whatever spiritual path we may choose to pursue, it is never an easy option. In recognizing the limitations of earthly existence and accepting our inevitable mortality, we are required to sacrifice a superficial, worldly perspective for a greater reality. Renouncing self-centred actions or material indulgences for the benefit of others forms part of most religious traditions.

AZTEC
SACRIFICE
This illustration
from a 16th-
century codex
shows prisoners
of war being
sacrificed to the
Aztec god of the
Sun and war,
Huitzilopochtli.

The concept of sacrifice, whether it is meant on a literal or a metaphorical level, has long been associated with religious traditions. Animate or inanimate objects have been offered to the gods for millennia in exchange for power, fertility, plentiful food supplies or victories in battle. Many faiths explicitly demand that their followers renunciate ordinary, habitual values.

Sacrifice

This is graphically exemplified in the Hebrew Bible's story of God's command to Abraham, first of the three patriarchs of the Jewish people, to sacrifice his son Isaac. In preparing the sacrifice, Abraham places the honour and love of God above natural human laws; he is rewarded by divine intervention and the substitution of a ram for the child.

In Christian belief, the Son of God himself provides the sacrifice through which humankind's salvation is achieved. A worshipper wishing to follow Christ, according to St Matthew, must make a personal abdication of worldly values.

FALL AND REDEMPTION
Giovanni da Modena's 15th-century depiction of the Crucifixion (right) shows Christ hanging from the Tree of Knowledge, the cause of Adam and Eve's expulsion from the Garden of Eden.

INCA SACRIFICE
Llamas (left) were among the Inca's most prized sacrificial animals. When there was a new moon, herds were taken to mountain tops and offered to the Sun god, Inti.

SICKNESS AND HEALING

Although modern medicine defines health as "freedom from disease", the word originally meant "wholeness", and comes from the Anglo-Saxon root that also gave us the word "holy". Medicine, spirituality and magic were once viewed as limbs of the same discipline, but modern scientific medicine has become distanced from its archaic beginnings.

In ancient times, sickness was seen as a punishment from the gods; witchcraft, demons and evil spirits were also thought responsible for medical problems. The exorcism of evil spirits played an important role in the ministry of Christ, who was able to cure conditions ranging from blindness to insanity.

Western medicine has its roots in the teachings of Hippocrates, a Greek physician who lived *c.*460–370 BCE. At that time, the deities Hygeia and Asklepios represented two different approaches to healing. Hygeia's followers believed that

MEDICINE MAN
Many modern drugs are based on age-old herbal remedies. In this contemporary painting of a medicine man by Gayle Ray, the healer is surrounded by plants, which are the tools of his trade.

Sickness and Healing

the role of medicine was to help the body use its own innate powers of healing to cure itself. Many therapies used today, from the Eastern and Western systems of healing, come under Hygeia's rule. Scientific medicine comes under the rule of Asklepios, who represented the belief that the physician's chief purpose was to treat the symptoms of disease caused by accidents or infections.

One of the chief roles of shamans and so-called "witch doctors" is to treat illness in the community. Chant, dance, prayer and powerful hallucinogenic drugs are used to provoke visions that reveal the causes of and cures for sickness. If the diagnosis is loss of soul, the shaman will attempt to find the patient's

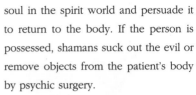

Sickness and Healing

CHINESE TRADITIONAL MEDICINE

Some of the main centres of energy in the body are illustrated in this ancient Chinese medical diagram.

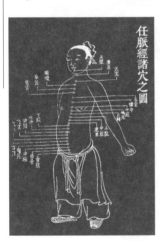

soul in the spirit world and persuade it to return to the body. If the person is possessed, shamans suck out the evil or remove objects from the patient's body by psychic surgery.

Many traditional schools believe that the body has the power to heal itself if the correct energies are accessed. In Chinese medicine, doctors rely on acupuncture – the gentle insertion of thin needles along special lines, termed meridians, on the body – to effect changes in the flow of energy to specific organs.

Most modern healers believe that their role is to address the fundamental imbalances that cause our bodies to fail – the deep spiritual roots of disease – while leaving scientific medicine to clear the more obvious, physical symptoms of illness that the body's own systems have failed to heal.

FEAR OF DEATH

The knowledge that we will die is the only certainty in our lives. In recent times, however, many societies have become distanced from death. Leaving the care of the elderly and infirm to experts, we try to halt our own bodies from ageing. So the prospect of dying remains a source of primal terror.

Death fascinates and repels almost all cultures. Some form of *memento mori* ("reminder of death") features in many religions, emphasizing the transience of material existence compared to the life of the soul. In Hindu and Buddhist Tantra, meditation in the charnel ground, or graveyard, is viewed as a way of going beyond terror – adepts deliberately seek out horrifying situations in order to transcend revulsion

THE GRIM REAPER
The scythe-bearing skeleton harvests the souls of the dead.

Fear of Death

and fear. Only among the decaying corpses is it possible to accept fully the inevitable dissolution of the body.

Representations of death often show its connections with life. The Hindu mother goddess Devi is both a loving provider and, as Kali, the destroyer who gathers in the bodies of the dead.

Such vivid depictions of death challenge the reluctance of many cultures to acknowledge its inevitability. Death is often viewed as a threatening stranger, as in the enduring Western image of the Grim Reaper, whose scythe shows his association with the natural agricultural cycle of death, or decay, and renewal.

The judgment of the soul after death is integral to many religions, although the nature, severity and length of punishment for transgressions varies. Interpretations of Christianity made from the 5th century until relatively recently stressed that it was impossible to achieve redemption from hell. Fear of death was made more intense by the

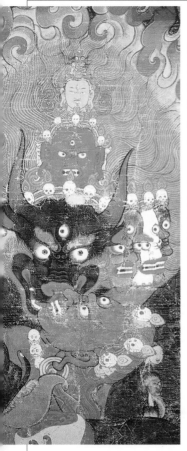

belief that sins committed during life would be punished for eternity. Medieval descriptions of hell told how intense despair and extreme pain would be experienced in its realms.

Eastern religions generally see the realms of hell as temporary stations in the cycle of death and rebirth. The Tibetan Lord of Death, Yama, judges the deeds of the newly deceased soul. If a person's actions are deemed to have been lacking or evil, his or her soul will be tortured until all guilt has been expiated. However, the victim need not fear the Lord of Death if he or she can see the essential emptiness of both him- or herself and the deities. The soul's suffering can thus be seen as self-created, and can be removed by recognizing the true nature of the hallucination.

Fear of Death

YAMANTAKA
This Tibetan *bodhisattva* helps those trapped in suffering, or hell.

CONFRONTING DEATH

Despite our understandable fear of the unknown, our need to recognize and accept the reality of death is an essential element of our development. From a spiritual perspective, death is an every-day, inevitable presence which gives sharper focus to our experience of life; by contrast, modern secular societies seek to minimize its significance.

Spiritual philosophers have tried for centuries to help others accept death's inevitability. The Daoist master Zhuang Zhou described the folly of ignoring death through the example of a man disturbed by his own shadow. He tried to run from it, but the more he ran, the more the shadow kept up with him. He ran faster and faster until he dropped dead. He did not realize that if he stepped into the shade and sat down, his shadow would vanish.

Christian beliefs are rooted in the conviction that the death and resurrection

CHRIST ON THE CROSS Images of the Crucifixion, such as this 15th-century painting by Rogier van der Weyden, remind Christians that Christ died to redeem their sins, offering them the possibility of resurrection.

Confronting Death

of Christ offer hope of immortality to every penitent soul. Contemplation of Christ's Passion, through either stylized representations or the symbol of the crucifix, is an important aspect of the faith which brings the believer into direct confrontation with agonizing physical death.

The rituals surrounding burial and mourning give spiritual guidance during an acute confrontation with death. Traditionally, family and friends prepare a corpse for cremation or burial and often undertake periods of ritual mourning, reflection and prayer. After a funeral, Jews observe seven days of mourning, during which the continuation of the deceased's soul is symbolized by a burning candle.

Many spiritual traditions have sought to provide the dying with descriptions of the soul's passage after death. In ancient Egypt, extracts from the Book of the Dead – a compilation of sacred spells – were buried with the wealthy and included images of the deceased overcoming trials in the underworld. The

Tibetan Book of the Dead describes death as a moment of piercing luminosity, or white light, before the soul begins its journey toward rebirth or liberation.

For many centuries, confronting death was a way of facing a beginning as well as an end. The large body of European medieval literature on the subject, the *Ars Moriendi* or Art of Dying, sought to enable the Christian soul to overcome diabolic forces and reach paradise. By unflinching acceptance of the reality of death during life, the soul is able to blossom into its full maturity.

Confronting Death

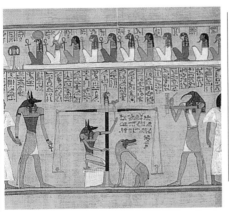

BOOK OF
THE DEAD
In this judgment
scene from an
Egyptian papyrus
of the 14th cen-
tury BCE, the
heart, or con-
science, of the
scribe Hunefer is
weighed against
a symbol of
justice and truth.

SURVIVAL OF THE SOUL

THE TERRA-
COTTA ARMY
More than 6,000
life-size terracot-
ta warriors were
buried with the
Chinese emperor
Shi Huangdi
(259–210BCE) to
protect him in
the afterlife.

As we grow older and our bodies become weaker, we gradually withdraw from the physical world. For those who have had time to prepare for their death, the parting of the body and soul can be a smooth and peaceful transition. Others suffer an untimely or violent departure, sending shock waves through their families and communities. The rituals surrounding death may offer comfort to those left behind and aid the soul's journey in the afterlife.

One of the most widely held beliefs in the East is reincarnation, which in its simplest form is the conviction that at death the soul travels from the old body to a new one. Buddhism offers a more complex perspective, teaching that the soul is not an unchanging entity, but that it is the inherent energy of the subtlest levels of consciousness that takes new life. An analogy often used to explain re-incarnation is the lighting of a

new candle from one that has burned down. The force that drives rebirth is known as *karma*, the law that whatever action is carried out in a previous life will have a corresponding result in the next. Spiritual progress through correct action will eventually lead the spirit toward *nirvana* (see page 245) and release from the cycle of rebirth. At his own death, known as *parinirvana*, the Buddha is believed by worshippers to have achieved the perfection of complete and final extinction.

DEATH AND
THE DEVIL
A Mexican wood
carving of
Death dancing
with the Devil.

The Hindu religion also affirms that the soul, or *atman*, transfers smoothly from one body to another after death, when consciousness sleeps. Rather than praising past deeds, the Hindu funeral liturgy addresses the soul directly,

FOOTPRINT OF
THE BUDDHA
After the Buddha
had meditated
through the
stages of his final
extinction, his
presence was
represented by a
pair of footprints.

Survival of the Soul

encouraging its progress to another body as the pyre burns.

This is in contrast to the ancient Egyptian practice of mummification, which sought to provide a permanent body for the *ka*, one of the elements into which the soul was believed to divide after death. After mummification, rituals were carried out to re-animate the dead person's faculties so that the *ka* could see, hear, smell, breathe and eat; all the sustenance needed for life was provided in the tomb.

The beliefs on survival after death vary in different cultures, but there are few religions that countenance a total extinction; most offer a purpose to individual existence through the enduring life of the soul.

THE COUNT DE ORGAZ
El Greco's *The Burial of the Count de Orgaz* (1586–8) shows St Augustine and St Stephen laying the count in his tomb – a reward for his generosity to the Church.

SEX AND GENDER

Many primal myths explain the creation of the cosmos as the joining together of male and female. Some cultures see the creation as resulting from a breach or a split, so that what was one became two. In both cases, the fundamental act of creation centres around the complementary opposites of male and female.

KRISHNA AND
THE MAIDENS
The solicitous
maidens in
this painting
of *c*.1710 are
worshippers
who desire
to be united
with the Hindu
god Krishna.

Sex and Gender

THE CORNUCOPIA
Meaning "horn of plenty", the cornucopia (left), both phallic and hollow, symbolizes the productive union of male and female.

THE UNICORN
This mythical beast (below) is both a symbol of female virginity and, through its horn, of physical or spiritual penetration.

Sex and Gender

THE SUN AND
THE MOON
To alchemists,
the two (above)
were symbolic of
the male (solar)
and female (lunar)
principles.

HERMAPHRO-
DITES
The myth that
humankind was
created by a
divine hermaph-
rodite was wide-
spread. This stat-
ue (right) of a
young hermaph-
rodite is Roman .

IMMORTALITY

THE SCARAB
In ancient Egypt the scarab was a symbol of renewal and regeneration linked with the Sun's passage.

We have tended not to inflict the humiliation of decay and death on our gods and goddesses, preferring instead to imbue them with the qualities of perpetual youth and beauty that we so yearn for ourselves. In myth, mortals often acquired eternal life by eating food and drink normally reserved for the gods. In the modern age, some people have opted to have their bodies frozen after death, hoping that regeneration will be possible in the future.

THE HARE
In this 18th-century Chinese embroidery (right), a hare, a symbol of longevity and fertility, is shown mixing the elixir of immortality.

THE PHOENIX
A symbol of resurrection and immortality in many cultures.

THE CRANE
In China, cranes (such as the one in this late 18th-century embroidery) were said to live for 1,000 years or more.

FORMS OF THE SPIRIT

The unseen presence of the soul or spirit animates the natural world. Various descriptions of the spirit liken it to wind, smoke or vapour. Comparisons to a shadow or reflection express the view that the soul dwells in a similar, parallel universe. Images of the soul are often connected with air and flight, and many cultures believe that, at death, the soul leaves the body in the shape of a bird or winged being. In medieval Christian iconography there are various symbols for the Holy Spirit, including a dove.

Forms of the Spirit

THE FALCON
In ancient Egypt, the falcon represented the soul's flight after death.

BIRD–WOMAN HYBRIDS
In Greek myth, these creatures (right) were linked to the theft of souls.

THE *BA*
In ancient Egypt, a *ba*, or spirit-being, was said to emerge from dead bodies.

A CHRISTIAN VIEW
In this panel from a 15th-century work by Simon Marmion a naked, pure-looking soul is being raised by two angels.

THE DOVE
In Christianity, the dove is often a symbol of the breath of God.

Forms of the Spirit

NATURE AND THE SOUL

Spirituality has been associated with the natural world since ancient times, when the power of the elements impacted directly upon human existence. Early hunters venerated the qualities of the animals they slew, and fertility rituals revered divinities to ensure the growth of essential crops. The physical forms of the Earth, as well as forests, rivers and other living features of its landscape, have long been regarded as sacred sites, expressing the presence of spirits or the creative authority of God. Modern lifestyles have distanced many of us from the natural world, and some believe that only tribal cultures retain a true spiritual appreciation of their environment.

The Sacred Earth

The Sacred Earth

Many of us sense that the Earth we inhabit is in some way sacred. In religious traditions, it is a manifestation of a vital divine power – every crevice and undulation, every spring and river, is infused with spiritual meaning. We may also find comfort through our affinity with the environment, and recognize that respect for the natural world is essential to our individual wellbeing.

Different landscapes carry their own spiritual identity. Many native peoples, such as the Maori of New Zealand, the Aboriginals of Australia and the inhabitants of Papua New Guinea, perceive in the Earth's relief indications of their ancestor spirits' presence and activities. Physical signs at

MOUNT SINAI
The lost peak where, according to the Bible, God spoke to Moses.

sacred sites, such as the marks of foot-prints or bodily impressions in the rocks, bear witness to the spirits' progress.

Some cultures have fashioned their own spiritual symbols out of the Earth. The man-made earthwork in Ohio created by Native American peoples more than 2,000 years ago is thought to be an effigy of the divinity known as Horned

The Sacred Earth

THE GREAT SERPENT
The striking Great Serpent Mound in Ohio, USA is a 1,250-ft (380-m) long, snake-shaped earthwork.

Serpent, which guarded sources of life, such as water, emerging from the Earth. Constructed in the form of a huge, uncoil-ing snake with an egg in its mouth, the effigy has obvious fertility associations.

Many early peoples believed that the physical surface of the Earth represented the body of a mother goddess (see page 20). Stones are still considered by some nomadic and hunting tribes to be protruding "bones". Gods and spirits were believed in many cultures to speak through cracks in the Earth's surface, which were often the sites of sacred oracles.

Rising toward the heavens, mountains have long been seen as the home of the gods and served as altars. They have also featured in most belief systems as places of vision and higher consciousness. Mount Fuji, in Japan, is held in the Shinto religion to be the physical embodiment of a *kami*, or divine spirit. Mountains also provide the setting for direct communication with God in the Jewish and Islamic religious traditions. Their slopes offer a natural place for contemplation that enables us to feel closer to the spiritual world.

MOUNT FUJI
The snow-capped mountain in the background of this 19th-century painted fan is Mount Fuji. Japan's most sacred peak, people climb it as an act of worship.

SPIRITS OF NATURE

For our ancestors, the recurring events of the natural world were divine in origin. Early peoples venerated the power of nature spirits and gods, seeking to preserve and explain the seasonal cycles that sustained life. We may believe ourselves removed from the immediate impact of a bad harvest or a late spring, but most of us are moved by the manifestations of nature, such as a beautiful sunset or a violent thunderstorm, that continue to link us to the moods of the Earth.

Cultures that revere nature often perceive mutability as a natural feature of their environment. Some may recognize no gulf between the souls of humans and other creatures; a tribe's ancestors may be glimpsed and worshipped in animal form. The dual nature of a shaman enables his or her soul to manifest itself

MAIZE
This silver head of corn, dating from the 15th or 16th century, reflects the reverence in which the Incas held their staple crop, maize.

Spirits of Nature

within an aspect or creature of the living world – the wind, a fish or a bird – in order to travel through water or air.

Aspects of humans, plants and animals combine in nature spirits, who represent an amoral, untamed power beyond any human order. In Europe, the Green Man, a spirit of lawless, burgeoning vegetation, still features in many seasonal festivals. Pan, the ancient Greek god of flocks and herds, also embodies wildness. The god's unseen presence, revealed by the eerie music of his pipes, was said to cause sudden disorientation and fear; the word "panic" describes the effect on humans of such an encounter.

Many early nature gods had two aspects: a shining summer form and a darker, underworld aspect of winter. Ishtar, the Akkadian goddess of love, war, fertility, childbirth and healing, was

Spirits of Nature

BACCHUS
The Roman god of wine and ecstasy, Bacchus (Dionysus to the Greeks) represented the wild side of nature.

Spirits of Nature

joined in sacred marriage with Tammuz, the god of growth and fertility. Tammuz was killed with the harvest every year. The grief-stricken goddess then followed her son-lover to the underworld, leaving the Earth in winter's grip: her miraculous return with Tammuz in the spring was celebrated as a divine miracle. For peoples dependent on the harvest, the annual re-emergence of deities such as these was essential to survival.

SHINTO CHARMS
These good-luck charms (below, left) on a Shinto shrine are for the attention of local gods (*kami*), believed to govern the natural world.

THE LIVING LANDSCAPE

PANORAMA
OF VARANASI
Many thousands
of Hindu
pilgrims visit
Varanasi each
year to bathe
in the waters of
the Ganges, the
most sacred of
Hindu rivers.

Certain sites in the natural world possess a strange, perhaps spiritual, charge, which we can sense. These are often places of ancient worship, where the *anima loci*, or "spirit of the place", was venerated as a local deity. Living features of the landscape – rivers and waterfalls, forests and sacred groves – were believed to harbour spirits or gods

The Living Landscape

who might bring power or protection to those who honoured them.

Water is essential to all life and, especially when clear and running, a recurrent symbol of the soul. Consecrated water is frequently used in rituals, such as the Christian rite of baptism, to bring about healing, cleansing or spiritual awakening. Many of the most sacred Hindu sites lie along the shores of the Ganges. The river is believed to be the personification of the goddess Ganga and to carry the essence of divine female energy in its waters. Drinking and washing in the Ganges are important Hindu rituals, attracting thousands of pilgrims to the sacred sites of Varanasi, Allahabad and other holy centres.

Water often also provides a demarcation between the realms of the living and the dead. The ancient Greeks considered rivers such as the Acheron, which flows partly underground, to be connected to the underworld. Springs, associated with creativity, purification, fertility and regeneration, are thought in many cultures to be sacred openings to realms beneath the Earth.

Trees have also been invested with spiritual significance since earliest times. In Angola, the Herero people believe the Omu-mboro-mbonga tree to be the place of origin of the first humans. Rituals surround the Life Tree of the Nepalese shamans, a solitary pine in which the shaman must endure a test of spiritual aptitude. Hindus revere the banyan tree for its longevity and powers of regeneration, and sacred shrines are often located at the banyan's base. The sounds of wind blowing through a tree's leaves have long been interpreted as the voices of gods and spirits, contributing to the spiritual power of forests and groves.

TREE SPIRITS
Spirit figures sculpted out of a tree trunk guard this holy well dedicated to the goddess Oshun in Oshogoo, Nigeria.

The Living Landscape

FERTILITY

Fertility has always been viewed as one of life's greatest blessings, whether it relates to our capacity for conceiving children or to the Earth's ability to sustain plants and animals. From earliest times, rituals evolved to ensure the fruitfulness of land and sea by honouring appropriate spirits and deities. Many of our religious spring festivals still re-affirm our profound connections with the natural world.

Surviving folk customs and artefacts shed light on the ways in which early civilizations maintained the health and harmony of the land. Ancient stone carvings of the mother goddess, known as "Venus figures", are archetypal symbols of fertility, honouring a nurturing and protective Queen of Heaven and Earth. Her womb was seen as the vessel of creation from which all sustenance flowed. A powerful fertility goddess appeared as Inanna in Sumer, Cybele in Anatolia,

Gaia and Demeter in Greece, the Magna Mater in Rome and Isis in ancient Egypt.

The sacred marriage of the goddess and her consort was re-created in fertility rites around the world. Across Europe the May Queen was symbolically married to the Green Man in a ceremony to promote the Earth's renewal. In Ireland, the king was obliged to marry a white mare, who represented the deity of the land.

Fertility

THE GREEN MAN
A European fertility figure, the Green Man was said to control the rains.

One widespread fertility custom was a form of ritual orgy. This usually took place in the spring, when the Earth could be made fruitful by a couple having intercourse in a ploughed furrow. Ritual copulation could also be used for more directly personal gain. At Cerne Abbas in southern England, a naked male figure cut into the chalk was seen as a potent source of fertility – childless couples sought to conceive by making love on top of the giant.

Fertility

Prayers for fertility are probably one of the oldest personal petitions to the gods. Many shamanic cultures believe that there is a limited number of souls in the world. If a woman is unable to conceive, she may ask the shaman to find a soul for her child, as her infertility could be caused by a lack of availability.

The main crop of an agricultural community was frequently venerated as a deity. Blood sacrifices were often made to these gods, because blood was perceived by many cultures to be a kind of soul substance, capable of generating new life. The Mayan peoples of Central America, whose staple food was maize, worshipped the crop as a god, in whose

TLALOC
The Aztec rain deity Tlaloc was also a fertility god, as the maize harvest was dependent on his sending sufficient rain.

honour the nobles of their kingdom let blood by piercing their tongues, earlobes and genitals.

CERES
Roman goddess Ceres (Demeter in Greek), who was believed to protect the crops.

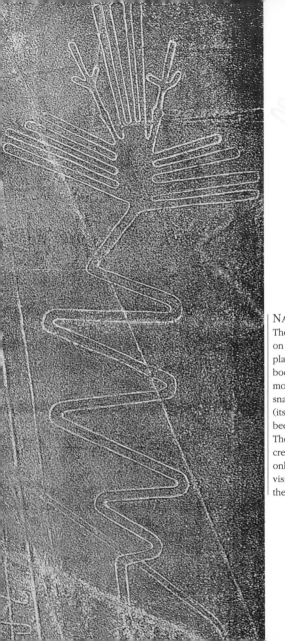

NAZCA LINES
These markings on the Nazca plain outline the body of an enormous bird with a snake-like neck (its head has been defaced). The complete creature could only have been visible from the air.

LINES OF FORCE

Humankind has recently embarked upon an unprecedented exercise to alter the face of the Earth. We have felled forests, drained marshes, diverted rivers and constructed a massive network of roads. But beneath these scars, the Earth's own energy still flows along its ancient, deep and mysterious courses.

At those places where the Earth's spiritual pulse can be felt most acutely, our ancestors often built enigmatic structures or carved vast images. Some of the most mysterious markings on the planet are on the Nazca plain in Peru. These are immense drawings of geometric figures, spirals, whales, condors, flowers and fantastic creatures, some of them more than 1,000 feet (300 metres) long. The artists who perfected these beautiful figures knew that the only way for them to be seen was from the sky. It has been suggested that the images were meant to be viewed by the gods, by souls ascending

Lines of Force

Lines of Force

after death, or by shamans in visions that they obtained during soul "flights".

The belief that paths of energy run through the landscape is the basis of the science of geomancy, which aims to harmonize human dwellings and activities with the physical and spiritual world. The ancient Chinese geomantic system known as *feng shui* recognizes and interprets the invisible energy lines that reach down from the sky into the mountains and through the ground. These energy lines fall into one of two categories: the positive, life-enhancing *chi* and the negative, perilous *sha*. *Feng shui* teaches that if a dwelling is properly placed, it will be in harmony with the land's energy, rather than blocking it.

St Michael Ley Line
The church of St Michael de Rupe in Brentnor, Devon, is built on a ley line linking St Michael's Mount in Cornwall to the abbey at Bury St Edmunds in Suffolk.

Belief in energy lines thrives still in the Western world. In 1922, businessman Alfred Watkins claimed to have "rediscovered" a system of "ley lines", linking many pagan (later, Christian) sacred sites in England. Aerial photography has revealed evidence of mysterious lines in the landscape. The longest such line in Britain links a series of churches dedicated to St Michael, the dragon slayer. A dragon's energy was believed to be fixed to the spot where it was killed, and the churches may be sited on pre-Christian shrines to the dragon's primordial power.

One of the most accepted ways of following a ley line or revealing the Earth's hidden energy is by dowsing. The dowser uses a forked stick, which is drawn irresistibly downward when it crosses underground water.

There is growing evidence that our ancestors were able to access the Earth's hidden energy. Many believe that if we can learn to do the same, much of the daily stress we encounter will disappear.

Lines of Force

SPIRIT OF THE HUNTERS

Our earliest ancestors were hunter-gatherers. Animals were an essential source of food; their skins were used to make clothing and their bones implements. The importance of the hunt is revealed in some of the oldest-known cave paintings, which depict animals such as bison and mammoth. These may have been painted as a magic spell to draw the animals to the hunters, or after a successful hunt to ensure that the animals' spirits returned to the Earth.

In hunting societies, the shaman ensured that an animal was killed according to the correct ritual. It was believed that animals gave up their bodies willingly to the hunter, as long as they and their spirit keepers were properly respected. If the correct ritual was observed, the animal's soul would return in a new body the following season. Among the Inuit in Alaska, it was believed that the Old Woman of the

DIANA
The Roman
hunter-goddess
(Greek Artemis).

Spirit of the Hunters

Seals provided fish, seals, walruses and whales to the people. If she was displeased, however, she withheld her bounty, and the shaman would have to visit her to try to effect a reconciliation.

Hunting depended on the acknowledgment of a spiritual affinity between the hunter and the hunted. Tribes who were heavily dependent on animals venerated certain species as their ancestors, and were prohibited from eating them.

Many ancient gods were worshipped in animal form. For example, a bear was the cult animal of the Greek goddess of the chase, Artemis.

Spirit of the Hunters

To the Celts, the hunt had associations with the Otherworld – and ancient myths told of enchanted animals luring hunters to the world of the dead. Later, in the Middle Ages, the stag became a symbol of the wandering pagan soul, lost in the forests of life and hunted by the holy servants of Christ.

Recently, the hunter has been increasingly portrayed as a bloodthirsty opponent of the spirit. In an age of animal rights it is hard to appreciate the mysterious connection between the hunter and the hunted that once conferred spiritual significance on the chase.

CERNUNNOS
Cernunnos, whose name meant "The Horned One", was the Celtic Master of Animals a god of nature, fertility and plenty who had strong links to the Otherworld.

DREAMTIME

AYERS ROCK,
AUSTRALIA
A sandstone out-
crop, Ayers Rock
(Uluru) is one
of the Aboriginals'
most sacred
sites. It is said
to have risen
from the flat
ground during
the Dreamtime,
as a monument
to an epic battle
between two
tribes of the
Sky Heroes.

When settlers from Europe first ventured into Australia's heartlands, they saw the Aboriginals who inhabited it as a "Stone-Age race", unable to adapt to modern life. As knowledge of their beliefs and customs has grown, however, the Aboriginals are increasingly seen as a people who have retained an important respect for the land, founded upon spiritual belief.

The Aboriginals believe that the world was initially unformed. Then, in the deep mythic past, during a time known as the Dreaming, Dreamtime or Creation period, the Sky Heroes appeared and lived on the Earth. These ancestors journeyed across the world, forming and naming every mountain,

Dreamtime

plain, river, tree, insect and animal. They also created the souls of every individual. The Sky Heroes left numinous traces of their presence in the landscape, which are constant reminders of the world's sacredness. The vast landmark called Ayers Rock, or Uluru as the tribal people know it, is a monument to an epic battle between two tribes of Sky Heroes. Every shape, hollow and boulder was formed as a result of this battle.

All Aboriginals can connect with the spirits by undertaking the Dream Journey. The journey's origins may lie in migratory hunting practices, but on a ritual level it is a way of renewing self-contact, the identity of the land being inseparable from personal identity. By visiting sacred places, which are known as hotspots, travellers repeat the world-creating events of the original Dreaming.

The Dreaming can also be recalled through rituals, performed on any piece of land. During these ceremonies, the

ABORIGINAL SHIELD
This pubic shield, made from shell, is inscribed with mythological figures.

men chant in a circle to the accompaniment of rhythmic music. The chants invoke the names and feats of the Sky Heroes, and continue until the spiritual energy is strong. Dancers then appear and re-enact the events of the Dreaming. At this point, all the participants in the ritual are said to have become Sky Heroes and are able to take part in the original mythic creation of the world.

In recent years, humankind has been forced to reassess its treatment of the planet. The ancient knowledge of the Aboriginals – that we are custodians of the Earth – is gaining recognition as a spiritually informed approach.

ABORIGINAL WANDERINGS Modern depictions of episodes from the Dreaming are, like the landscape itself, difficult to interpret. They may show the routes taken by the ancestors and sites that are imbued with their power.

Dreamtime

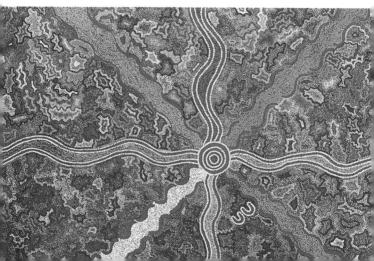

AIR

Air is the most intangible element, yet it is necessary to animate all living things; it is the natural medium of the invisible soul, filling the expanse that divides the heavens from the Earth. Those gods and goddesses who are believed to inhabit the air are generally of more recent origin than terrestrial deities and offered those who worshipped them freedom from the physical limitations of worldly existence. The complex symbolism that surrounds air tends to focus on related phenomena that are easier to envisage, such as the sky, wind, flight and breath.

WINGED CREATURES
This Jewish book illustration, dating from 1348, shows four winged creatures similar to those described in the Hebrew Bible by Ezekiel. They may be manifestations of God's spirit.

Air

PRAYER FLAGS
Prayers on these flags (above) are borne by the wind around this Buddhist *stupa* in the Katmandu Valley, Nepal.

ISIS
The Egyptian goddess (left) is sometimes shown with wings.

THUNDERBIRD
The Native American spirit (left) adorns this 19th-century drum.

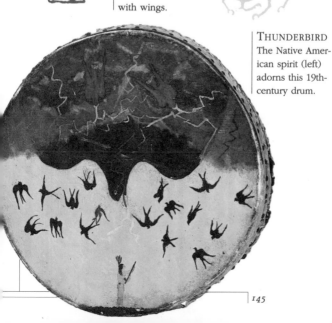

Air

PRANA
The vital force that is carried in the air, entering our bodies when we breathe, is symbolized by this central glyph (right). In India its name is *prana*, in China *chi*, and Japan *ki*.

THE ORACLE OF ZEUS
The Greek Oracle of Zeus (above) was a major source of divine knowledge. Answers to questions about the future were said to be conveyed by the wind rustling leaves.

FIRE

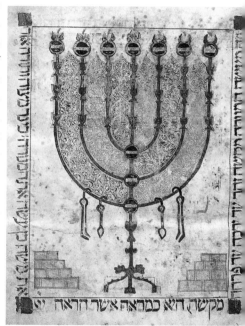

Since our earliest ancestors first learned how to make fire, the flame has been worshipped as the essence of divinity and the source of light. Fire is a complex symbol with many conflicting aspects; it can be creative or destructive, divine or demonic, providing gentle heat or devouring everything in its path. As a source of warmth and illumination, fire has often been seen as a symbol of the soul.

MENORAH
This Jewish candelabrum is an ancient symbol of spiritual light.

A SHIP FUNERAL
In Scandinavia, important members of society were often cremated in long-ships (above).

AGNI
Hindu god of fire, Agni (right), is an invincible warrior and a presence in the hearth of every home. He also devours the corpses in the cremation ground.

THE PASCHAL CANDLE

The candle (left) is a Christian symbol of Jesus as the "Light of the World" (John 8.12). Orthodox Christians announce Easter by the priest lighting the Paschal Candle in a dark church, and proclaiming "Christ is risen!".

RA-HARAKHTY

This ancient Egyptian stela of *c*.1000BCE portrays a woman worshipping the falcon-headed Ra-Harakhty – a manifestation of the rising Sun – who radiates beneficial rays.

Fire

EARTH

Earth

Traditional societies saw the Earth as a living being with a soul. The whole world was regarded as sacred: the creative powers of the universe were believed to direct the recurring cycles of the seasons, and spiritual forces were said to have shaped the very forms of the Earth's crust. Certain features of the landscape, such as rocks, mountains, caves, cliffs, islands and springs, were recognized as being the dwelling places of local deities.

STANDING STONES

Massive uncarved stones were erected across northwestern Europe in the period 3200–1500BCE. They may have had an astronomical or ritual purpose.

CAVE TEMPLES
Caves cut from rock express a desire for unity between the human spirit and the ancient body of the Earth. These ancient Buddhist cave temples (below) are in Maharashtra, India.

PETROGLYPHS
Prehistoric drawings or carvings on rock – such as this mythical being found near Peterborough, Ontario (above) – may mark the sites of physical or spiritual events. They may also be invocations to the gods.

Earth

DIAMONDS AND JADE
A hard diamond (above) symbolizes eternity and jade (below) is revered in China.

TAURUS
In astrology, the bull (above) is the strongest and most fertile of the three Earth signs.

RUBIES
These blood-red gemstones (left) have been seen as symbols of royalty, power and passion.

SILVER AND GOLD
Dense and precious gold (left) represents the rays of the Sun. Silver (below) has lunar, feminine associations.

WATER

VISHNU AS MATSYA
The Hindu god Vishnu's first incarnation was as Matsya, a fish.

A universal symbol for the soul, water has traditionally been invested with magical properties. Many sites with water were believed to be the dwelling places of gods or supernatural beings, and were seen as sources of both physical healing and spiritual transformation. Cleansing in steam or baptism in running water often symbolizes a return to purity, washing away the old life to be born anew.

Water

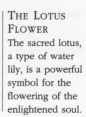

THE LOTUS FLOWER
The sacred lotus, a type of water lily, is a powerful symbol for the flowering of the enlightened soul.

The Fall of Babylon
The city became a metaphor for excess human ambition and Christian commentaries on the biblical Apocalypse (above) depicted the city's sins being washed clean.

The Baptism of Christ
The New Testament describes how Jesus was baptized in the River Jordan by his cousin, John (right).

A VIEW OF PARADISE

The Islamic vision of paradise (above) consists of a series of luxurious gardens irrigated by four rivers radiating from the centre.

SACRED ANIMALS

Sacred Animals

Animals have been regarded as sacred symbols since earliest times. Hunter communities invested their quarry with spiritual significance, and the hunts themselves were sometimes viewed as acts of veneration of the gods. Deities of ancient religious traditions were often represented in animal form: the association of the Mother Goddess with lions has probably existed since Paleolithic times. Some cultures discovered animal forms in the skies in the constellations. Animals also played an important physical role in religious ceremonies. Birds' and animals' movements were studied to divine the future, and the favour of the gods was sought through offerings of sacrificial beasts.

BASTET
Egyptians saw cats as manifestations of the benign feline goddess Bastet, linked with sex and motherhood.

IMAGINARY BEASTS

This illustration (right) from a medieval Spanish manuscript shows Christ enthroned in majesty surrounded by angels and four beasts, whose features have been taken from various animals.

A BEAR DRUM

To the Haida people of British Columbia, bears are powerful spirit helpers. A bear decorates this drum (below), used by a Haida shaman to summon spirits.

Sacred Animals

BIRDS
A Melanesian
carving of a sky
being. Flight and
the ascent of the
soul have long
been linked, and
deities often take
the form of birds.

THE IMPERIAL DRAGON
The Chinese
imperial dragon
(right) symbol-
izes the Emperor,
wisdom, the
rising sun
and rain.

BEES
The communal
organization of
bees, from
collecting pollen
to guarding the
hive, have made
them symbols of
diligence.

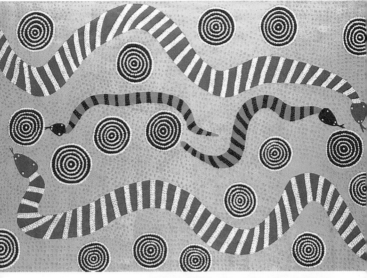

SNAKES
The Rainbow
Serpent is the
Aboriginals'
most important
ancestor.

THE
SACRED COW
A white cow –
considered
sacred by Hindus
– decorated for
a festival.

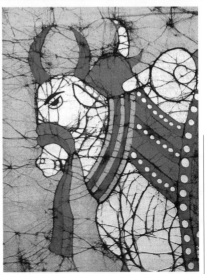

Sacred Animals

MITHRAS AND THE BULL

The Persian god Mithras (above) became the centre of a Mystery Cult during the Roman Empire. Mithras was usually portrayed slaying a great bull, which symbolized his animal nature.

GARUDA

Half-man and half-bird, Garuda is the vehicle of the Hindu god Vishnu. He is depicted in this 18th-century painting (right) carrying his master and Vishnu's consort Lakshmi, the goddess of prosperity.

THE SPIRIT WORLD

Most of our spiritual traditions acknowledge the existence of realms beyond the material world. Some beliefs consider these realms to be accessible only after death, when the soul is liberated from the constraints of a physical body. Others, especially those of shamanic cultures, regard voyages between realms as possible in life – often achieved in dreams or trance states, and assisted by spirit helpers. The proximity of spiritual and physical worlds, especially at certain times of the year, has an ambiguous aspect in many faiths. The spirit world may be represented as a source of sacred knowledge, comfort or healing wisdom. However, travel to another realm is seen as a dangerous business, which, whether undertaken in life or after death, requires informed spiritual preparation.

Soul Realms

In our spiritual beliefs, many of us are drawn to the idea of existence beyond the material world. Our conception of such realms, in which the soul escapes the limitations of a physical body, may be shaped by religious tradition or by our own imaginings and experiences.

The human realm is generally placed in the middle layer of the spiritual universe, with the heavens above and an underworld, usually associated with the souls of the dead, below. The World Tree (see page 24) often links the different cosmological tiers and in some cultures offers the possibility of moving between them. Water also provides a traditional demarcation of different realms, and crossing over water is a complex symbol, associated with forms of spiritual rebirth.

The Buddhist Wheel of Life can be interpreted as a map showing states of mind or as a literal guide to other worlds – all potential places of rebirth. The

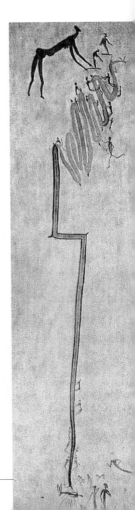

Wheel's lower spokes depict the realms of animals, hungry ghosts, and several regions of hell, whose inhabitants are subjected to terrible torments. In contrast to other religions' eternal hells, the tortured souls will eventually be released through the Buddha's compassion, and will be reborn elsewhere. Even the heavenly realm of joy, set at the top of the Wheel of Life, is subject to mutability. Buddhist gods are also held in the endless cycle of rebirth.

The Christian concept of heaven combines the astrology and cosmology of ancient Greece and Rome with Jewish images of the Lamb. It presents a vision of God and Christ enthroned, surrounded by saints, elders, angelic hosts and the

Soul Realms

THE WHEEL OF LIFE
The six sections of this Tibetan Buddhist Wheel of Life (above) represent realms of rebirth.

SKY SPIRIT
A tree grows from a woman sacrificed to an African sky spirit (left).

165

A JAPANESE GHOST
A 19th-century Japanese woodblock shows a terrifying ghost return for vengeance on his murderers.

multitude of the redeemed. The heavenly realm offers believers a prospect of eternal, immutable bliss, in contrast to the finite, material realm of the Earth, which will be destroyed in an eventual Apocalypse. Yet in Judaism the relationship of the "World to Come" with the material world is less clearly defined. The sacred Jewish writings in the Talmud contain many references to the soul's afterlife. Whether the World to Come is to be seen as a separate realm, or whether it describes a resurrection of the dead in this world, depends upon the individual believer's interpretation of the Talmud.

SPIRIT HELPERS

The idea of leaving our physical world for an uncharted spiritual realm arouses fear of the unknown in all of us. Even cultures that believe that the soul regularly visits other realms during its time on Earth regard these wanderings as dangerous, particularly for those without special knowledge or guidance from personal spirit helpers. The shamans of North America or Southeast Asia frequently undertake "soul flights" to the spirit world in search of healing wisdom or a lost soul. On such journeys, the shaman depends upon spirit helpers to ensure his or her safety and success.

The belief in a form of benevolent

THE ANNUNCIATION
In this 15th-century painting by Fra Angelico, the Virgin Mary is told by the angel Gabriel that she is pregnant with the Son of God. God is often said to communicate through angels.

Spirit Helpers

spirit is integral to shamanic practice. However, the notion also occurs in many other systems of belief. Angels (see pages 188–189) assume the role of intermediaries between God and human beings in several religions, appearing in dreams to sound warnings or give advice. The Hebrew Bible names only Gabriel and Michael, who respectively reveal the future and combat the forces of evil. In Christian tradition, every individual is described as having his or her own protecting angel. The Koran describes several instances of the Prophet Muhammad's encounters with angels. In one of the

GRIFFINS
A griffin is the mythological offspring of an eagle and a lion. It is said to guard the Tree of Life or the path to salvation.

ANCESTOR
SPIRITS
*The Spirit of
the Dead Keeps
Watch*, painted
by Paul Gauguin
in 1892, portrays
a Tahitian woman
lying on her bed.
She is watched
over by an older
woman in black,
possibly repre-
senting her
ancestor spirit.

most famous, Jibreel (Gabriel) brought
the Prophet a winged mule with the face
of a woman. Jibreel then accompanied
Muhammad, mounted on the mule's
back, on a miraculous journey in which
they ascended into the heavens. Here
the Prophet was instructed by the Voice
of God before returning to Earth.

The philosophers of ancient Greece
also drew upon the concept of spirit
helpers. According to Plato, every human
being possessed a spirit, or *daemon* – a

Spirit Helpers

fiery spark from the original world soul. Every *daemon* had the power to guide or instruct, but its advice could be heard only by those pure of spirit.

Shamans may gather an astonishing variety of helper spirits during their long apprenticeship. Guardian spirits usually reflect the nature of the land: those of the Inuit peoples, for example, may be water creatures, such as seals or walruses. Shamans from the rainforest tribes often use plants with narcotic powers to achieve their visionary trances and transform themselves into a jaguar, fish or bird. For many of these *vegetalistas*, plants such as the hallucinogenic *ayahuasca* are thought to be spirit teachers. By ingesting the qualities of these spirits, the shaman's own identity merges with that of the helper. Yet a degree of separation remains, and the spirits need to be respected if they are not to abandon the shaman or even become malign.

STEALERS OF THE SOUL

Almost all spiritual traditions consider our souls to be essentially vulnerable. Without careful instruction and preparation, they may become lost on the voyage to the underworld, or afterlife. Demons, anxious to steal human souls for their own purposes, have appeared in all cultures, whether as pernicious external influences or more sophisticated manifestations of our unconscious minds.

The human world is often perceived as infused by malign, benevolent or amoral spirits from another realm. In the Shinto religion, the *kami* who govern most aspects of nature and human existence include *oni*, or

ST ZENO EXORCIZING AN EVIL SPIRIT In this painting by Francesco de Stefano Pesellino, a Christian bishop is portrayed exorcizing a woman by commanding her evil spirit to abandon its possession in the name of Jesus.

Stealers of the Soul

Stealers of the Soul

demons, who may cause many problems for humans. Some *oni* assume the form of animal spirits that are able to possess humans; if this occurs, the *oni* must be formally exorcized by a priest.

The need to create spiritual boundaries

in response to this perceived threat manifests itself in the rituals of several cultures. Protected space, such as sacred sites of worship, is defined by the uncontrollable forces outside it – the province of ghosts, demons and evil spirits seeking to capture living souls. Such creatures often represent the souls

LUCIFER
Lucifer is one of the many guises of Satan, the Judeo-Christian adversary of God. This painting by Alexandre Filho shows Lucifer, tied to a lizard.

VOODOO CHARM

Devotees of Voodoo, a religion widespread in Haiti, believe that the world is populated by *loa* (spirits), who may favour, or harm, humans. Charms are carried to ward off evil spirits.

of human dead, unable to leave the physical world, perhaps because of evil actions undertaken in life. Various sacred rituals, such as the Hindu period of *pitrpaksha*, attempt to contain or negate the influence of deceased souls. In Africa, when those who have died are eventually forgotten by their descendants, their spirits become unknown ghosts who, if harnessed by sorcerers, may cause harm to the living.

Physical and mental illnesses have long been attributed to supernatural causes. Many traditions possess rituals of exorcism designed to release the weakened soul from a malevolent power. Inexplicable diseases of the mind, such as epilepsy, were particularly feared, and associated with diabolic possession. The Gospels of Mark, Matthew and Luke include instances of exorcism as part of Christ's healing ministry, and the formal rite is still included in Christian doctrine.

Healers of the Soul

DREAMS AND VISIONS

Since Sigmund Freud published *The Interpretation of Dreams* in 1899, the images that we experience while we are sleeping have been widely regarded in the West as subconscious references to our past. For thousands of years, however, dreams were believed by many cultures to be the most common vehicle for divine revelation.

Some societies believe that during sleep the soul enters a parallel world, which is as real and meaningful as our waking existence. In Malaysia, Senoi children are told that dream monsters have no power to hurt them unless they flee. They are taught to cultivate "dream friends", who

THE VISIONS OF EZRA

Seven visions received by the Prophet Ezra from the archangel Uriel are related in the Apocrypha, an appendix to the Old Testament.

help them conquer such adversaries. These friends might give the child a gift, such as a poem, to bring back into consciousness with him or her. Upon waking, the child is encouraged to recite it.

When dreams were frequently understood to have been sent by the gods, their interpretation was of great importance. The earliest records of dreams, incised on clay tablets and collected into interpretive dream books, were produced in Babylon and Assyria at the end of the 4th millennium BCE.

In ancient Egypt, people seeking divine guidance would take herbal medicines before sleeping in the temple. On waking, their dreams would be interpreted by the priest. This practice of dream incubation was adopted by the Greeks, who built more than 300 shrines to serve as dream oracles. Because dreamers believed that they were visited by the gods, the sick frequently went to the shrines, hoping to be aided by Asklepios, the god of medicine.

Dreams and Visions

Dreams and Visions

VISHNU
DREAMING
This 17th-century
painting shows
the Hindu god
Vishnu dreaming
on the back of
the serpent
Ananta between
the destruction
of one world
and the creation
of the next.

Divine revelation by means of dreams and visions provides a common thread through many of the great religions. In the Hebrew Bible, dream sequences play a prominent part in the stories of Jacob and Joseph, which tell of the founding of the 12 tribes of Israel and their migration to Egypt. The Koran is believed by Muslims to be the literal word of God, transmitted to the Prophet Muhammad in a series of visions. The

birth of Christ is heralded in a dream to his father Joseph.

In the East, particularly in Buddhist and Hindu thought, sleep was seen as a type of consciousness similar to that experienced after death. It was said that in the dream state, an extremely fluid "mental body" existed which was not tied down to physical laws and could therefore have a wide variety of experiences.

In the West, the role that dreams can play in providing access to our inner thoughts and desires has been the subject of much recent study. Carl Jung taught that, while dreaming, people may encounter ancient symbols, called "archetypes", that have remained active in the unconscious mind. Some psychologists believe that the depression and "loss of soul" which are so widespread in modern civilization are in fact the response of the mind to loss of contact with the religious in modern life. Dreamwork is a way of re-establishing that contact.

Dreams and Visions

COMMUNICATING WITH THE GODS

In many of today's native cultures, it is believed that the gods are active in reaching out to the human realm. They may show themselves in the power of elemental forces, the movement of the heavens or the growth of crops; and their immanence gives inspiration and meaning to rituals of worship. The direct intervention of deities in human affairs informed several early religious traditions, from the Greek gods' participation in the Trojan wars to

THE STIGMATA
In this 13th-century fresco by Giotto, St Francis is shown at the moment of receiving the stigmata, the marks of the five wounds inflicted on Christ during the Crucifixion.

the divine status accorded to ancient Egyptian pharaohs. The manifestation of the divine has also entered into all the major monotheistic beliefs. Yahweh, the God of the Hebrew Bible, reveals himself through miraculous actions, such as parting the Red Sea to allow the Israelites' passage. In Hindu tradition, the seventh and eighth avatars of Vishnu – Rama and Krishna – appeared on Earth to defeat evil and restore harmony; their victories are celebrated in the sacred texts of the *Ramayana* and *Mahabharata*.

Modern religions seek to communicate with their gods through prayer, petition and praise. The smoke of incense, for example, is thought by Daoists to transport prayers up to the gods. Other belief systems rely on the mediation of a spirit community. Shamanistic beliefs recognize

Communicating with the Gods

PRAYER
WHEEL
Each time the
wheel turns,
the Buddhist
prayer written
on a scroll
inside is dis-
seminated.

A SHAMANIC
DRUM
Drumming is
frequently
undertaken by
shamans to sum-
mon the spirits.

spirit powers everywhere in their environment: the Inuit sea spirit, known as
Sedra or Nuliajak, governs the sea and
sends out animals for the hunt, while
Sila, the air spirit, controls rain, wind
and snow. The spirits are feared by the
Inuit as sources of foul weather and mis-
fortune in hunting. Attempts to placate
them include ritual incantations and the
wearing of masks and amulets.

The imperial sacrifices to heaven
conducted by Chinese emperors in the
Temple of Heaven in Beijing sought to
communicate directly with the spiritual
realm. The emperor offered prayers for
a successful harvest in his capacity as
heaven's representative on Earth.

Hinduism perceives the physical
realm to be infused with a divine presence. Simple shrines appear by
the wayside in both the towns
and the countryside. Such
shrines facilitate impulsive
communication as well as
longer worship.

TURNING-POINTS OF THE YEAR

In acknowledging the closeness of spiritual and material realms, we emphasize the importance and sacredness of the border regions between them. Many traditions have used certain moments of transition in the year as a focus for our relationship with other worlds.

In Celtic belief, the boundaries between the seasons were periods when divisions between the different realms became permeable. The festivals of Beltane and Samhain were celebrated respectively in the spring and autumn, the seasons of the year held to be most auspicious for divine supplication. The night before Samhain, the Celtic New Year, is now known as Hallowe'en – it is still viewed as an occasion when normal demarcations are suspended. The doorways between the spirit world and the material world were thought to open, admitting both the souls of the ancestors

HALLOWE'EN
Jack-o'-lanterns
are a relic of
the bonfires that
were once lit on
the last day of
the Celtic year.

Turning-Points of the Year

181

and, potentially, evil spirits. Fires and lights in the home were traditionally extinguished at Samhain. Sacred flames were taken from bonfires lit on mountain tops (see page 33) to rekindle hearth fires, restoring light and protection.

The Hindu festival of Divali, which marks the New Year for many communities, uses firework displays to celebrate the regenerative triumph of light over darkness. Restless spirits must be propitiated, and the god of death, Yama, pacified; cows, too, are honoured as symbols of fertility and prosperity.

New Year is seen in many spiritual traditions as the time for sweeping away all the accumulation of evil from the old year. This process is celebrated in ritual purification – extinguishing fires, fasting, and expelling demons or evil spirits. The concept of the scapegoat – an effigy who symbolically assumed the sins of an entire community, and who was then slaughtered or cast out into the wilderness – recurs in several New Year ceremonies.

PERILOUS JOURNEYS

Voyages that involve great danger are a common theme in world religions and mythology. Many believe that such journeys are an allegory for the progress of the soul: that it is only through leaving behind all worldly attachments that we can learn our true worth, and that we must conquer our deepest fear – often death – if we are to achieve serenity.

Many cultures have tales of gods and mortals visiting the underworld to try to defeat death. The Greek myth of the musician Orpheus, who visited Hades to try to win back his wife Eurydice, is mirrored in the Shinto tale of the deities Izanagi

A DAOIST MAP OF THE UNDERWORLD This Daoist map from 12th-century China shows the nine purgatorial chambers of the soul in the underworld.

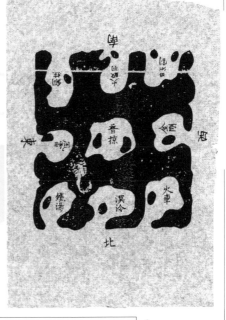

Perilous Journeys

Perilous Journeys

and his sister and wife, Izanami. When Izanami died giving birth to the God of Fire, her grief-stricken brother journeyed to the Land of the Dead to retrieve her. When he looked at his sister's decaying face, however, he fled in horror.

Perilous journeys rarely resolve themselves as the traveller wishes or expects. In the Epic of Gilgamesh, the Sumerian hero visits the underworld to learn the secret of eternal life. However, the plant that offers everlasting youth is eaten by a serpent, and Gilgamesh returns home accepting his mortality. In the Celtic Voyage of Bran, the hero and his 26 companions are lured to the underworld. When they eventually return to Ireland, the first man to set foot on land crumbles to dust. Bran learns that 300 years have passed since they set sail.

Many traditions claim that the underworld borders ours and can be entered through a cave-mouth, lake, volcanic crater or barrow mound. Others tell of a land located beneath the ocean or beyond the seas. The Chumash people in California believe that the Land of the Dead is separated from this world by a body of water: the soul must cross the bridge, avoiding water monsters on the way. Preparation for death while living – in the Chumash's case, by participating in hallucinogenic rituals – is believed to increase the soul's chances of making a successful transition to the underworld.

JOINING THE DEAD
The belief that the underworld was bounded by water is portrayed in this ancient Greek fresco, which shows a newly released soul diving toward the realm of the dead.

Angels

ANGELS

Deriving their name from the Greek *angelos*, meaning messenger, angels have traditionally been intermediaries between spiritual and human realms. They feature in the Jewish, Christian and Islamic faiths, bringing divine revelations, as well as intervening in human affairs and acting as guardians. The heavenly beings are divided into nine choirs, or hierarchical orders, ranging from seraphim, who are in direct communication with God, to angels, who are closest to humankind.

THE ARCHANGEL GABRIEL Like Ariel, Uriel and Michael, Gabriel was an archangel. In Islamic belief Gabriel (Jibreel) heralded the revelation of the Koran to Muhammad (left).

Angels

CHOIRS OF ANGELS The celestial hierarchy or "choir" of angels has often been artistically interpreted in musical terms. Hans Memling's 15th-century painting *Five Musical Angels* (above) portrays the harmony of heaven.

HEAVEN

THE PEACEFUL
KINGDOM
Dora Holzhan-
dler's image
(below) of the
biblical heaven.

The belief that a just and devout life enables our soul to enter paradise after death is the promised reward of most Western religions. Heaven in the Bible or the Koran is usually portrayed as a garden filled with peace, beauty and love. However, each of us also has a deeply personal concept of the afterlife, which may change during our earthly lives. Some visualize a happy land filled with loved ones who have gone before; others believe that they will become part of a great cosmic energy. Many Eastern religions describe several heavens, which form temporary homes to the gods and deserving humans.

ANGEL OF THE
APOCALYPSE
This 13th-century
Italian fresco
(left) depicts the
distinctive fiery
seraph with three
pairs of wings.

Heaven

**BUDDHIST
HEAVENS**
This mural shows
the Buddha in
the Tavatimsa

Heaven. Buddhists
believe there are
six heavens in
the first sphere
of existence.

STAIRWAY
TO HEAVEN
Many people who
have had near-
death experiences
have described
ascending stairs
(below).

MUHAMMAD
ASCENDING
TO HEAVEN
This illustration
(above) depicts
Muhammad riding
a winged animal
to heaven, where
he received the
commandments to
pray from Allah.

HELL

In early cultures, hell was simply the abode of the souls of the dead. As such, it was a shadowy, subterranean world, ruled by the dark lord of death. The ancient Greeks believed the dead went to Hades, a vast cavern inside the Earth.

The concept that hell was reserved for those who had led a sinful life emerged later, culminating in the Middle Ages with the Christian Church's graphic descriptions of punishments meted out to sinners.

CHRIST'S DESCENT INTO HELL
This 17th-century Russian icon shows Christ, having died, descending into hell to deliver the righteous.

Hell

THE DAMNED
The Christian view of hell, as captured in this 15th-century altarpiece, was a dark prison where sinners were tortured for all eternity.

三殿宋帝王余

割舌　挖眼　　　　　剉骨

JUDGING THE DEAD IN HELL
A Daoist image shows the judge Guan Gong presiding over a court in hell. A report on a person's life is used as the basis for reward or punishment – such as torture by demons.

MICTLANTE-CUHTLI

Aztecs believed all souls passed through the god Mictlantecuhtli's (right) underworld.

AN ETHIOPIAN IMAGE OF HELL

Ethiopians imagine hell as a fiery realm (below).

SOUL AND TRANSCENDENCE

The pressures of our modern lives are focused primarily upon material success. Spiritual beliefs offer us an alternative vision of existence, in which the limitations of such a perspective are transcended by the potential of the soul. While faiths possess many different aspects, most belief systems seek to draw us into a more profound understanding of ourselves. The disciplines of meditation, prayer, retreat and vision quests demand perseverance and dedication, and a teacher's wisdom is often seen as essential in guiding us toward our spiritual goal. In attempting to reach an inexpressible absolute, whether it is called paradise, or *nirvana*, or a name more personal to ourselves, we pay tribute to the highest aspiration of the human spirit.

FAITH

Faith

Developing and preserving a spiritual faith may not be a comfortable path. In acknowledging our belief, we are often called upon to relinquish material success and rational, scientific beliefs to focus instead upon a deeper, more abstract reality.

Faith is particularly important in Judaism, Islam and Christianity, with their emphasis upon God's eventual judgment of each human soul. Faith is not a fixed concept, but may change in emphasis over time; in Judaism, for example, the Torah interprets faith to mean an immense trust in God, rather than – as now – a belief in his very existence. All three monotheistic religions believe that the divine presence is manifested through sacred scriptures, which record the history and nature of God's

SATIS
The handprints of Hindu widows who have died on their husbands' funeral pyres in the act of *sati*.

JONAH
Jonah is swallowed by a whale (right) when his faith in God fails.

covenant with his chosen people. Such texts are integral to the rituals and tradition that inspire personal belief. This individual spiritual faith is more than an intellectual conviction – it is a passionate, emotional commitment that may often be counterpointed by agonizing doubt.

The power of faith is indisputable: it has long inspired individuals to make great sacrifices. The Islamic obligation of *jihad* requires physical defence of the faith if necessary, without regard for personal safety. Many spiritual traditions celebrate those who confronted the challenges of their beliefs: Christian martyrs, for example, are often venerated as the recipients of divine strength and power.

The faith of many Eastern beliefs is less focused on divine textual authority. Even the most holy writings of Buddhism, for example, are considered mere indications of a truth that can only come from personal experience. In Hinduism, the spiritual goal of liberation from the cycle of rebirth may be pursued through knowledge, action or devotion. The third of these involves a complete surrender of the ego to the mystical experience of divine grace and power. Knowledge of the deity thus emerges through faith rather than itself inspiring spiritual conviction.

Faith and doubt are inextricably linked. The Zen Buddhist tradition believes that great faith, great doubt and great perseverance are needed to make spiritual progress. Faith is required to discover and trust the truth of Buddhist teaching; doubt to challenge superficial understanding; and perseverance to continue. In recognizing the complexities and hardships of a spiritual path, our religions and beliefs celebrate the enduring human determination to overcome them.

COMMUNION CHALICE
Transubstantiation, in which Communion wine is transformed into the Blood of Christ, is essential to Catholic faith.

Faith

The Defeat of Suffering

THE DEFEAT OF SUFFERING

We all encounter periods of misery that defy us to discover a deeper meaning or purpose in our lives. Most spiritual beliefs offer both explanations and solutions for our distress. Reconciling a universal order with the apparently arbitrary distribution of grief in the world is a challenge, yet we all know people who are able to accept suffering as a feature of existence and who accommodate it within a broader spiritual perspective.

In Hindu belief the individual soul is linked to the ultimate reality of *brahman*, the vital essence of the cosmos. Suffering arises from an inability to recognize the reality of *brahman*, along with an excessive

THE SCOURGING OF CHRIST
This painting by Giotto depicts Christ being scourged, or whipped, before his Crucifixion.

attachment to worldly wealth, pleasure and emotions. According to the law of *karma*, behaviour in one life will continue to have repercussions in future reincarnations. Through virtuous conduct and the defeat of egotism, the soul may advance through a series of lives toward spiritual perfection. If it cannot shake off material attachments, however, or continues to commit evil actions, it will remain permanently trapped in a spiral of suffering.

The Buddha's teachings emphasize our need to confront the reality of *duhkha*, meaning transience, mutability and decay, that essentially defines human existence. In recognizing suffering as an inescapable facet of our lives, Buddhists seek to transcend the craving for illusory pleasures and security that paradoxically anchors people more firmly in the miseries of the world. In Buddhism, the true defeat of suffering demands acceptance of its inevitability through meditation techniques that still the mind.

The Defeat of Suffering

THE BUDDHA
The Buddha's followers believe they can only escape suffering by attaining *nirvana*.

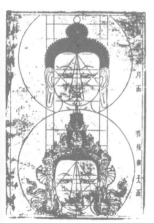

Judaism, Islam and Christianity all acknowledge the existence of earthly suffering within the dominion of a just and all-powerful God. This paradox is partly explained by the concept of the divine retribution or reward that will be meted out to the individual in a life after death; the Jewish Talmud contains many references to such redress. However, Judaism ultimately recognizes suffering to be rooted in divine mystery, and thus beyond the scope of human rationalization.

Christianity perceives Christ's suffering on the Cross and subsequent resurrection to be the divine response to human misery. By sharing in the feelings of anguish endured by Christ, a believer may be brought closer to the Godhead. Transient suffering on Earth is set against the hope of an enduring redemption.

PENITENCE

As well as adhering to the law of the state, each of us follows a personal code of behaviour and sometimes also a set of religious rules. If we break any of these rules, we may be haunted by guilt. Many find that by feeling remorse for our past sins or mistakes, we allow the healing power of penitence and atonement to enter our hearts and purify our spirits.

The importance of recognizing and confessing one's sins, and of being forgiven, has long been acknowledged in the Judeo-Christian tradition. The Jewish calendar features an annual season of penitence, marked by important festivals. The liturgy of Rosh Ha-Shanah, the Jewish New Year, focuses on the kingship of God. The festival is the first of ten days' penitence, during which time true repentance is said to be especially acceptable to God. The tenth day is Yom Kippur, the Day of Atonement.

THE JEWISH *SHOFAR*
The *shofar*, a ram's horn, is sounded on Rosh Ha-Shanah, marking the start of the Jewish New Year and heralding the ten days of penitence and the Day of Atonement.

Penitence

In the Roman Catholic Church, early
forms of penance – the forgiving of sins
after baptism – involved sinners making a
public confession and incurring severe
penalties. Because penance was allowed
only once, those guilty of serious sins
would often put it off until death neared.
In the light of this, in 1215 the system of
confessing to a priest at least once a year
was introduced. Later, harsh punishments
were commuted to prayers or donations.

Abuses of the confessional were
instrumental in causing the Reformation,
and today most Protestants make a
standard congregational confession at

DYING MAN
This 17th-century painting shows a dying man. Islam teaches that Allah forgives those who truly repent.

morning or evening prayer. The Anglican version reads: "We have left undone those things which we ought to have done; and we have done those things we ought not to have done ... ."

VISION QUESTS

Vision Quests

Most of us at some point feel that our lives lack purpose, but few of us seek, or desire, to be given a task by the divine. However, there are some (shamans, mystics and great teachers) who have crossed the threshold between the physical and the spiritual worlds, seeking salvation for themselves and others. The search for spiritual knowledge or revelation is known as a vision quest and may involve life-endangering practices such as fasting, drug-taking, self-mutilation and blood-letting. Those on a quest might learn a song with special meaning, see a vision of

THE HOLY GRAIL
This illustration (above) from a 14th-century Flemish manuscript shows Josephe, the son of Joseph of Arimathea, conducting mass before a Holy Grail quest.

the future of the tribe, or find inspiration to lead others on their spiritual journey.

One of the most famous Western vision quests is the legendary search for the Holy Grail. Believed to be the chalice used by Jesus at the Last Supper, in which Joseph of Arimathea later collected the blood of Christ, the Grail first appeared in medieval French stories associating it with King Arthur's court. In later tales, the knights of the Round Table pledged to search for the Grail and then embarked upon a series of trials from which many did not return. The trials, set by mysterious figures along the way, sought to test the worthiness of each knight's soul, and to expose the conflict between worldly attachments and a true love of God. Only four knights – Lancelot, Perceval, Bors and Galahad – succeeded in seeing the Grail and only Galahad participated in its mysteries. The Grail quest is still a resonant symbol of the soul's search for spiritual salvation.

JAGUAR
Amazonian shamans identify with the jaguar (below), and assume its form on vision quests.

Vision Quests

Vision Quests

Many of the major religions owe part of their central message to their founders' vision quests. After his baptism, the New Testament relates how Christ wandered alone in the desert for 40 days and 40 nights. Having refused to be tempted by the devil, he returned with a new vision for humanity. Muhammad too went alone into the hills, where the archangel Jibreel (Gabriel) told him that he was to be Allah's messenger. The Prophet then spoke what Muslims believe to be the words of Allah, as recorded in the Koran.

Vision quests are also an important feature of Native American culture. Shamans communicate with the spirits after fasting and bathing in a sweat lodge. Returning from their interior journey, they bring back counsel and healing for the tribe.

A SHAMANIC VISION QUEST This yarn painting (right), made from dyed wool, was produced by western Mexico's Huichol people. It depicts the spiritual journey of an antlered shaman.

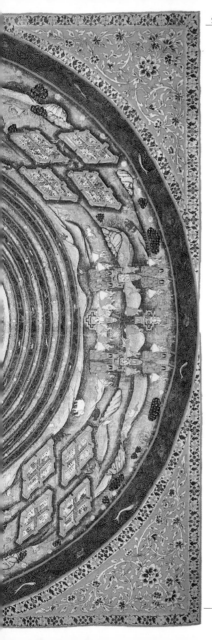

TOWARD NON-ATTACHMENT

Eastern spiritual traditions emphasize the solitary path of the wandering ascetic or *sannyasin*, a person who has retired from society and devoted himself or herself to spiritual realization through meditation and surrender. The search for the *atman*, or soul, begins by withdrawing into the "cave of the heart". *Sannyasin*s abandon all attachments, such as family ties, power, money,

THE JAIN UNIVERSE
A diagram of the Jain universe with the World Axis at its centre.

Toward Non-Attachment

Toward Non-Attachment

ambition and even existing religious duties. Hindus encourage and support these wandering holy men and women, as they believe that the mystic is to the community what the soul is to the body, giving it life and inspiration.

Both the Buddha and Mahavira, the respective founders of Buddhism and Jainism, were renowned ascetics. While the Buddha taught the Middle Way between materialism and renunciation, Mahavira believed that release from the endless cycle of rebirth required complete abandonment of the material

THE TRANS-CENDENTAL RAINBOW
In Hindu and Buddhist Tantra, those who have overcome the poverty of their ties on Earth are said to have attained the highest meditative state possible – that of the rainbow body.

world. From the moment of his renunciation he went naked and showed no interest in food, water or sleep.

The great monastic houses of Christian Europe imposed strict vows of poverty, chastity and obedience on those who took holy orders. For some this was a life of torment, while for others it offered a gateway to total freedom of the spirit: confronted with the absolute love of God, all worldly concerns slipped away. St John of the Cross urged contemplatives to seek to enter into Christ's being in complete nakedness, emptiness and poverty.

This renunciation of the spirit would have been understood by the ancient Daoist sages of China. They believed that to act in accord with the *Dao* (the Way), people needed to discover stillness of heart, to overcome ceaseless desire and ambition, and to live in harmony with nature. Many sages renounced all wealth and ambition to live in the mountains among the clouds and pine trees. Here they cultivated supreme non-attachment, their mirror-like minds reflecting a parade of phenomena, but retaining nothing.

Toward Non-Attachment

MEDITATION

Meditation

The Sufis – Islamic mystics – say that knowledge without spiritual practice is like a tree that does not bear fruit. The discipline of meditation allows the practitioner to live more fully in the present moment with awareness and peace. Religious traditions teach many different forms of meditation. However, recalling the mind from its habitual chaotic turmoil to quietness and solitude – "the still point of the turning world" – is central to all.

Meditation, or *dhyana*, is the penultimate limb of Raja Yoga, one of the most famous Hindu philosophical traditions. It was first written down in Patanjali's *Yoga Sutra*. The mind is likened to the surface of a lake ruffled by the wind.

KALI *YANTRA*
The Hindu goddess Kali is at the centre of this *yantra* (above), a sacred diagram used as a focus for meditation.

HATHA YOGA
This 18th-century illustration (right) depicts a Hindu ascetic performing a posture recommended for meditation.

Meditation

The purpose of yoga is to cause the wind to subside and allow the waters to return to stillness. Using meditation, we are able to settle down the myriad thoughts that splinter our concentration, and so are left with a clear picture of our true self and our place in the world.

In Christian mysticism there is a tradition of formless meditation – the aim of which, according to St Francis, is to achieve "a loving, simple and permanent attentiveness of the mind to divine things". Mystics of this tradition aspired to be in the presence of God, rather than becoming one with God. St John of the Cross said that the soul should be allowed to remain in rest and quietude, in which, through patience and perseverance, without any conscious activity, the presence of God would be found.

Meditation can bring relief from the continuous whirlpool of our thoughts, offering the soul an ability to live fully in the present moment, and to discover a deep delight in the everyday world.

SHRI *YANTRA*
The Shri Yantra is the archetypal *yantra*. Its pattern evokes the sacred union of Shri, a manifestation of the goddess Shakti, with her male aspect, Shiva. The *yantra* is composed of nine triangles. The dot at the centre symbolizes the Absolute.

PRAYER

When we pray, we are petitioning, or communing with, the divine, perhaps in search of inspiration, guidance or comfort. Prayers may also be said in response to fear: when in great danger, many who consider themselves atheists find themselves praying.

The simplest prayers are those that ask for assistance during important episodes in our lives, such as childbirth, coming of age, marriage, war and death. In many cultures – for example, in ancient Greece – there were a great number of deities to whom one could pray, each of whom had an area of responsibility. Nike

CHRIST PANTOCRATOR Orthodox Christians pray to icons such as this one.

Prayer

would be invoked for victory in war, Poseidon when crossing the sea, Hera for easy childbirth, and Demeter for an abundant harvest.

In Eastern religions, such as Hinduism and Jainism, *mantra*s are used in prayer. The *mantra* is a short word or syllable (such as "*Om*") that encapsulates a form of cosmic power and is therefore considered sacred. The word *mantra* has the Sanskrit verb *man* (to think) as its root, and as an instrument of thought it is used to protect the mind from wandering into its usual discursive channels.

The Eastern Orthodox Church places a strong emphasis on meditative prayer. One of the most familiar supplications, the Jesus Prayer, is used in a way similar to a *mantra*. The words are simple: "Lord Jesus Christ, Son of God, have mercy on me, a sinner." Apparently an ordinary form of petitionary prayer, this formula was used to effect changes in the consciousness. The prayer was said aloud for a specific number of times, then repeated silently at intervals during the day and night. Finally, the prayer was taken down from the "head' centre of consciousness to the "heart" centre where it was thought to live with every heartbeat. In monasteries, monks would repeat the prayer while counting knots on a cord.

Rosaries are used as an aid to prayer in many of the world's religions. Sikhs repeat the divine name, *nam*, while counting the beads on a rosary; Muslims say one of the 99 names of Allah that appear in the Koran while turning their prayer beads; members of the Pure Land sect of Chinese Buddhists use a rosary when reciting the name of a deified Buddha such as Amitabha; and Christians, particularly Roman Catholics, say prayers while counting the beads of their rosary.

ISLAMIC BEADS
One of Allah's 99 names is recited for each of the 33 prayer beads in the chaplet (opposite), which is turned three times.

A MALE ASCETIC
This mid-17th-century painting (below) from Rajasthan portrays an ascetic at prayer.

Prayer

RETREAT

Retreat

As the stresses and distractions of modern life increase, many of us find that we lack the necessary space and calm for spiritual growth. By making regular visits to monasteries, ashrams or other places of religious retreat, we are responding to an inner call for solitude to restore the balance between the sacred and secular in our lives.

The first Christian hermits retreated to the Egyptian desert during the 4th century CE, fleeing persecution. There they lived simple lives of prayer and meditation in loosely organized communities. Many of the monks fasted, and some attempted more rigorous feats of endurance – such

A MAP
OF MOUNT
ATHOS
The first Orthodox community on the Mount Athos peninsula in Greece was established c.961. By the 14th century there were 40 monasteries, 20 of which are still in use.

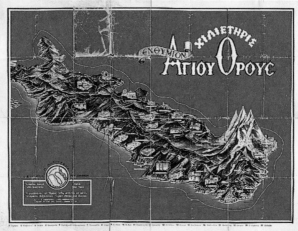

as living at the top of columns or walling themselves up in caves – to try to detach themselves from the physical world. St Isaac of Syria explained their motives by saying: "A man who wishes to become excellent in God has first to wean himself from the world ... "

Following in the footsteps of Muhammad, who spent long periods meditating alone in the desert, many Sufis – members of a sect of Islamic mystics – considered retreat to be the most important of all spiritual disciplines. Early Sufis believed that every person had a human and a divine soul which competed for nourishment. It was only by denying the human soul, through renunciation of the pleasures of life, that the divine soul could flourish. A Sufi would often stay in his cell for several weeks, repeating Allah's name continuously. It is said that some Sufis obtained sudden illumination almost immediately,

MILAREPA
This 17th-century Tibetan statue depicts the hermit yogi Milarepa (1040–1123). He started his career as a magician and became a great Buddhist *lama* (teacher).

Retreat

Retreat

others after some weeks, but the retreat was judged to be successful only if the vision remained undiminished after the Sufi had re-entered everyday life.

Devotees of Tibetan Buddhism on a retreat often seek desolate places in the mountains. One of the most celebrated Tibetan Buddhist saints was Milarepa, who achieved total enlightenment after a period of living alone in a state of near-starvation in the caves of the Himalayas.

Milarepa never became a monk, but many who did also carried out extreme forms of retreat. A Buddhist monk could be walled up in a cell for years, cultivating his inner vision so that at death, when the mind and body separated, he would not be in a state of bewilderment, and so could be sure of a favourable rebirth.

Although retreat does not suit every spiritual seeker, many great saints such as Milarepa overcame the human need for society; they found that solitude gave them the psychological space in which to further their spiritual development.

CHRISTIAN TROGLODYTES Early Christian monks hollowed out churches, chapels and small cells in the volcanic rocks of the remote Anatolian region of Cappadocia.

ECSTASY AND TRANSFORMATION

Life teaches us that many advances are inspirational. Although most religious traditions emphasize the importance of a gradual spiritual development through prayer or meditation, they recognize that ecstatic or visionary states can lead to sudden leaps in faith or understanding. Such states can be self-induced, by taking hallucinogenic drugs or listening to mesmerizing sounds, or may also occur spontaneously.

St Teresa of Avila was renowned for her ecstatic visions: she said she was visited by an angel whose face seemed to be aflame. The angel plunged a fiery golden arrow into her heart, leaving her aflame with the love of God. The physical power of St Teresa's raptures could raise her whole body from the ground. She

ST TERESA
A flaming angel appeared in St Teresa of Avila's ecstatic visions.

Ecstasy and Transformation

Ecstasy and Transformation

taught that the mark of spiritual under-standing was not the degree of bliss that a person experienced or how much he or she loved God, but how much he or she was able to love other people.

Many religious traditions see altered states of consciousness as stages on the spiritual path. The value of transcendent states is that they provide a powerful vision of reality beyond day-to-day con-sciousness. Those who enter a transcen-dent state may experience a pleasant change in their sensory perceptions. Maharishi Mahesh Yogi, the founder of the Transcendental Meditation (TM) movement, taught that the energy released during such blissful states, if properly channelled, could liberate human consciousness.

In shamanic societies, trances or ecstatic states are entered in order to seek help and advice for the tribe from the spirit world. The shaman journeys on a magical flight, which may have been achieved by spiritual means alone,

DIONYSUS
This mosaic of
*c.*180CE is from
the House of
Masks on Delos.
It shows Diony-
sus, the Greek
god of wine and
altered states,
riding a leopard.

or may have been induced by drumming, dancing or taking hallucinogens. On the journey, the shaman has a transformed vision of reality; if successful, he or she may gain knowledge of the life-force that pervades the universe.

The mistrust felt in many modern societies toward altered states of consciousness also existed in ancient Greece. There, when people were drunk, acting or in a state of religious ecstasy, they were believed to be in the realm of Dionysus, whose rites were associated with excess and madness. The god's most famous followers were the bacchantes, a band of frenzied women who were said to tear apart animals and humans during their orgiastic revels. Today, most of the religious traditions that include ecstatic practices remain outside the mainstream, and the value that can be gained by entering a transcendent state is often questioned in the light of the dangers that can be involved.

Ecstasy and Transformation

TEACHERS OF FAITH

Teachers of Faith

LAO ZI
This 16th-century
Chinese carving
depicts Lao Zi,
who is credited
with founding
Daoism.

Many of the world's religious traditions require us to develop great spiritual knowledge and understanding to overcome obstacles on the path to enlightenment. Most of us need a skilful teacher to direct, stimulate and encourage our commitment. Under their experienced guidance, we begin to see beyond the realm of everyday concerns to a world of vast and profound wisdom.

Spiritual development in the major monotheistic religions – Judaism, Islam and Christianity – is linked to knowledge of sacred, divinely inspired scriptures. Each religion regards teaching as an essential function of its spiritual leaders. Modern rabbis, for example, combine the roles of preacher, pastor and counsellor with their scholarly study of the Torah – the sacred teachings of Judaism. The interpretation of the Torah's message is seen as a never-ending task: creative discussion and argument are considered

Teachers of Faith

profound forms of worship. By contrast, Islamic teachers demand a rigid adherence to the Koran, which they believe contains the literal words of Allah. Religious devotion places great emphasis upon learning the Koran by heart, which forms the basis of Islamic instruction.

Christians regard Jesus as the supreme teacher, the inspiration for all preachers of the faith, and the Gospels as the vehicle through which his doctrines are expressed (often in the parables and aphorisms that characterize Jewish teaching).

Spiritual teachers are viewed as extremely important in Hinduism – they set devotees on the paths of knowledge, devotion and action toward the ultimate goal of *moksha* (liberation from the cycle of rebirth). The paths of knowledge and devotion

CHRIST AND HIS APOSTLES Christ's first 12 disciples were chosen to spread his message. Judas, who betrayed Christ, is absent from this 13th-century image (left).

are usually undertaken with the guidance of a *guru* – a personal spiritual guide who advises and assists throughout the student's journey.

Buddhist teaching is structured upon the formulation of the Four Noble Truths recognized by the Buddha on his enlightenment. As the Buddhist tradition developed, the role of the teacher changed. The first *arhats* or "worthy ones" – the spiritual ideal of the Theravada school – emerged from among the Buddha's original followers after his death. In the later schools of Mahayana Buddhism, strong emphasis is placed upon compassion, with the teacher taking a very personal involvement in the life of the student. By contrast, in the Vajrayana and Zen schools, compassion took on a fierce quality, using unconventional methods to force the student into experiencing reality directly. Many celebrated Mahayana and Vajrayana teachers are viewed as the incarnations of great *bodhisattva*s (see page 246), whose essence is enlightenment.

Teachers of Faith

BUDDHIST
*ARHAT*S
In the Theravada Buddhist school, *arhat*s – such as the two in this Tibetan image (above) – are enlightened beings who will never be reborn.

THE PATH OF RITUAL

Rituals, both sacred and secular, pervade every aspect of our lives, giving structure to our positive experiences of faith. Many rituals are re-enactments of a society's sacred myths, and so may contain symbolic forms or archetypes that communicate directly with our psyche or soul.

The Chinese philosopher Confucius believed that his society was in a state of moral decline owing to a general lack of ritual at all levels. Although no book of rites exists from Confucius's time, guidance is provided in the *Li Ji*, a text written after his death, on ancestor worship, mourning and sacrificial ceremonies.

Guru Nanak, the founder of Sikhism, believed ritual could impede communication with God. Sikhs do, however, recognize and celebrate five rites of passage: the birth of a child, the bestowing of a child's name, the coming of age, marriage and death.

As well as the ritual observances of prayer, fasting, alms-giving and pilgrimage, Islam recognizes two "official" Holy Days. 'Id al-Fitr, the Feast of the Breaking of the Fast, ends Ramadan. The most important day in the calendar, 'Id al-Adha, the Great Feast, celebrates Ibrahim's willingness to sacrifice his son Ishmael. On this day, every Muslim should ritually sacrifice a *halal* (lawful) animal such as a sheep, goat, cow or camel.

Many Jewish rituals originated with the 613 precepts of the Torah. Each of these divine commandments is known as a *mitzvah*. The obligation to keep the precepts begins when a boy reaches the age of 13 and a girl the age of 12, hence the terms Bar Mitzvah and Bat Mitzvah for the Jewish coming-of-age ceremonies. The Sabbath and the Passover, two of the most important Jewish rituals, are acts of thanksgiving. Each week, the Sabbath essentially celebrates the creation of the

The Path of Ritual

THE GREAT MOSQUE AT SAMARRA
The dynamic spiral minaret of the 9th-century mosque at Samarra in Iraq reflects the desire of the soul to ascend to the heavens.

Earth and remembers that God is present in everything. During the annual spring festival of the Passover, Jews give thanks for their safe delivery from Egypt. A ritual meal and service are held in the home on the first night of the Passover. Known as the Seder, it uses symbolic foods to remind Jews of their ancestors' ordeal.

The Christian Gospels all suggest that the Jewish Passover was associated in some way with the first Lord's Supper, when Christ directed his followers to commemorate him by eating bread and drinking wine. Since then, Christians have ritually consumed these ancient symbols of body and spirit in the Communion.

THE *SEDER*
*The Passover
Meal*, by Dora
Holzhandler,

depicts the meal
and service held
on the first night
of the Passover.

THE EXCEPTIONAL LIFE

Most of us have had contact with individuals whose spiritual knowledge is greater than our own. However, the really exceptional lives belong to those who found lasting systems of belief, based upon the personal quests they have undertaken to discover true spiritual values.

The Buddha, born in Nepal in the 6th century BCE, was such a person. He devoted much of his life to seeking an explanation of human suffering and finally achieved enlightenment beneath the Bodhi Tree at Bodh Gaya (see pages 42–43). His subsequent teachings of *dharma*, or

truth, offered to rich and poor alike, established an enduring legacy.

His near-contemporary Confucius established a spiritual philosophy in China that informed the country's beliefs for more than 2,000 years. Confucius emphasized that learning and moral development were both a personal responsibility and an ethical gesture of reverence to heaven.

Islam's founder, the Prophet Muhammad, was born in Mecca in 570 CE. Muhammad is believed to have been visited by the archangel Gabriel, or Jibreel,

DEATH OF THE BUDDHA This scene from a 17th-century Japanese hand-scroll shows the *parinirvana* (final extinction) of the Buddha. All those who remain within the cycle of rebirth – gods and demons, men and women, birds and animals – watch the event with humility.

The Exceptional Life

on whose command he began to recite the sacred words of Allah. He is honoured in Islam as Allah's human prophet, the vehicle of the divine word and proclaimer of the true faith.

Jesus, by contrast, is considered by most Christians to be both God and man. He offered radical teachings on achieving salvation through God's forgiveness, as well as preaching the need for compassion and love on Earth. In a climate of messianic fervour, Jesus's charismatic ministry and concern for the poor were viewed as dangerous by the authorities, leading to his Crucifixion.

MUHAMMAD AND HIS DISCIPLES
Traditionally, the prophet's face is veiled as a mark of respect, as in this illustration from a 16th-century manuscript.

PARADISE

Most of us believe that, in the present age, paradise cannot be attained while we are alive – although some say that it can be glimpsed. Many cultures agree, however, that humankind once dwelt in a luxurious paradise, close to the divine, and that our souls yearn to return there.

Paradise is usually described as a garden or park, often with a mountain at its heart and rivers flowing outward in the four cardinal directions. Existence there was invested with total harmony and peace, as well as with a glorious awareness of the sustaining divine presence. Descriptions of paradise served as an example of how life could be lived and also as a promise of the soul's reward for a virtuous life.

Paradise

ALI HUSEIN AND HASAN IN PARADISE
The two grandsons of the Prophet Muhammad are depicted in paradise in this 17th-century Islamic miniature.

Paradise

In the Koran, it is written that the Gardens of Paradise are divided into four sections – those of the Soul, the Heart, the Spirit and the Essence – and that each is watered by crystal streams, beside which the faithful recline, drinking wine.

In Hindu and Buddhist systems of belief, paradise is seen not as an ultimate goal, but as a temporary state, subject to the universal conditions of change and decay. The great Hindu gods

GARDEN OF PARADISE
This 16th-century German vision of paradise shows the Queen of Heaven in the Garden of Eden.

Paradise

Brahma, Vishnu and Shiva are not considered to be immortal but are thought to enter the Wheel of Time at the end of each *yuga* (see page 29). Mahayana Buddhism teaches that "Buddha fields" may be created through the spiritual power of a Buddha or an advanced *bodhisattva*. Buddhist devotees may be favourably reborn into these gardens of spiritual bliss, where progress may be made toward full enlightenment.

The Garden of Eden is associated with paradise in the Judeo-Christian tradition: Jewish prayers for the dead contain an entreaty that the deceased's soul should rest there in a state of immortal bliss. This closeness to God, lost since the Fall from Eden after Adam and Eve ate the fruit of the Tree of Knowledge, is viewed as the soul's reward after a lifetime's striving for perfection.

Many of the world's great mystical traditions understand that more than an actual location, paradise is a powerful symbol of peace within the human heart.

ENLIGHTENMENT

From our childhood, when the dark seems to be full of unknown terrors, we continue to acknowledge the power of light to conquer forces of darkness and evil. Many religions consider the ritual lighting of candles to symbolize spiritual transformation, from the darkness of ignorance and doubt to the revelation of living faith. In the Hebrew Bible, the Psalms often associate light with the soul's progress toward salvation – "thy word is a lamp unto my feet and a light unto my path". Enlightenment, literally meaning "being brought into the light", is the spiritual goal of many systems of belief – a deep clarity of perception in which truth can be comprehended through a conviction of both mind and heart.

In his quest for enlightenment, the Buddha sought a solution for the over-whelming presence of *duhkha* (roughly translated as impermanence and suffering, in all their diverse forms) in human

Enlightenment

life. He finally achieved enlightenment beneath the Bodhi Tree at Bodh Gaya in a single night. In recognizing the cycle of *samsara*, which chains humans to rebirth, the Buddha-to-be saw that as an individual's actions and their consequences were linked (the law of *karma*),

JOURNEY TO
THE CENTRE
The maze is
symbolic of the
inner journey
toward enlight-
enment. The path
is lit by the candle
of knowledge.

spiritually correct action over several lives was the key to achieving release from the cycle. This understanding brought him to the perfection of becoming a Buddha ("One who is Awake"). As the Buddha achieved *nirvana* (literally meaning "blown out", a state of being likened to the extinction of a candle), his accumulated wisdom was distilled into the Four Noble Truths and infinite compassion – both of which are at the core of Buddhist teachings.

The Buddha taught that anyone might embark upon the spiritual quest, and his early followers believed in four stages of enlightenment, ranging from an initial rejection of egotism and illusion to the ultimate realization of *nirvana* as an *arhat*, or "worthy one". Later traditions of Buddhism believed that the highest enlightenment lay in becoming a *bodhisattva*. The *bodhisattva* ideal, that of world saviour, vowed never to seek nirvana until even the grass and the dust had achieved buddhahood.

Enlightenment

SACRED FIGURES

Every world religion reveres those of its members who have shown great spiritual strength and dedication during their lives. The actions of such men and women have often been used as examples of what human beings are capable of achieving. Stories of the Christian saints, the holy ascetics of Hinduism, the ten gurus honoured by Sikhs, the Daoist immortals, Islam's mystical Sufis and the generous *bodhisattva*s of Buddhism, serve as inspirational models for others on the spiritual path.

MA GU
This Chinese painting on silk (above) by Hsiang Kun shows the Daoist immortal Ma Gu.

GURU NANAK
The founder of Sikhism, Guru Nanak (1469–1539, below, left).

CHRISTIAN EVANGELISTS
The four saints who wrote the gospels of the New Testament are depicted in the 8th-century *Book of Kells* as winged beasts (right).

Sacred Figures

ST CATHERINE OF ALEXANDRIA

In legend, St Catherine (left) is said to have lived during the 4th-century rule of Roman emperor Maxentius. She was tortured on a spiked wheel and beheaded for opposing the persecution of Christians.

AVALOKITESH-VARA

A popular Mahayana *bodhisattva*, Avalokiteshvara (below, left) is revered as the embodiment of compassion. He is usually depicted with multiple arms, with which he dispenses aid. The Dalai Lamas are sometimes said to be reincarnations of this *bodhisattva*.

MIRACLES

Myths and legends describe events that do not fit into the scientific, rational view of the world. Some stories are clearly allegories of the soul's journey, but others describe historical events in which the established laws of nature are thought to have been overturned. For generations, examples of prophecy, clairvoyance and out-of-the-body experiences have been reported. The thirst for marvels remains strong today, and stories of miraculous cures and heavenly visions still abound. Miracles have often been performed by spiritual leaders to assert their divinity or to reinforce their message.

Miracles

THE BIRTH OF
THE BUDDHA
Queen Maya
(above) is said to
have produced
the Buddha from
her side.

ASCENSION OF
MUHAMMAD
Angels (right)
escorting
Muhammad into
the heavens.

side running head

LAZARUS
St John's Gospel tells how Christ proved his power over death by returning Lazarus to life, as shown in this painting (above) by Giotto.

Miracles

FEEDING THE FIVE THOUSAND

Once, when preaching to 5,000 people, Jesus is said to have fed the crowd with just two fish and five loaves of bread.

THE BUDDHA WALKING ON WATER

In this panel (above) from the *stupa* at Sanchi, the Buddha is seen walking on water, a miracle he performed to convince his disciple Kashyapa of the truth of his message.

SACRED TEXTS

Although a few cultures still pass down their rituals and beliefs by word of mouth, most have a central text or texts that outline their history, laws and spiritual convictions. To avoid misinterpretation, there are authorized versions of sacred texts such as the Christian Bible, the Jewish Torah and the Sikh Guru Granth Sahib. Muslims believe that the Koran gives the actual words of God. All sacred texts are written in a highly symbolic form and are open to interpretation. They embody the sacred values of a culture and record the ancestry of the people and their precious relationship to the gods.

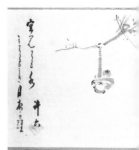

ZEN ART
Calligraphy and painting express the sacred (above).

THE KORAN
The Koran (below) is often embellished with ornate calligraphy.

THE HEBREW BIBLE

Jews revere the name of God, and although it may be written down, as in this page (above) from the Hebrew Bible, it is not usually read aloud.

THE DAO
This Chinese character (right) for the "Way" refers to the undefinable principle responsible for creation out of nothing.

THE CHRISTIAN BIBLE

The Christian Bible comprises the texts of the Old and the New Testaments. Before the advent of printing, manuscripts were copied out by skilled monks and were often highly illustrated, or illuminated. This example (left) shows the flight into Egypt of Mary and Joseph with the infant Jesus.

THE TORAH

A crown (left) is placed over each end of the Torah scrolls to symbolize the sovereignty of the Torah over Jews.

BELIEF SYSTEMS OF THE WORLD

AFRICAN (NATIVE) RELIGIONS

Those religions in Africa that were not introduced by Islamic or Christian missionaries are generally animist: that is, they perceive spirit beings in local landmarks and other natural features, although some tribes also acknowledge deities of a higher order. Most rely on the mediation of a shaman or holy person who is able to travel into the spirit world in a trance to seek out the solutions to current problems. Many tribes have their own creation myth, often featuring a vast, primal serpent.

ALCHEMY

Alchemy, which originated in ancient Egypt and ancient Greece, allies chemistry and astrology to seek not merely the marvellous physical medium that will turn base metals into gold, but also its metaphysical equivalent, believed to unlock the secrets of the universe.

ANCIENT EGYPTIAN RELIGION

The history of ancient Egypt spans more than two millennia (c.3000–300BCE). A number of elements remained constant in Egyptian religion, but were often given different names at different times: a creation story, involving the sky, the Earth, and the air between; the Sun god; the dualistic struggle between the good god Horus and the sometimes less virtuous god Seth; the mother goddess; and the afterlife. Deities often personified animals; many were specific to a region or city. From early on, the pharaoh was also accorded divine status. Egyptian religion was in the hands of a powerful and wealthy priesthood.

ANCIENT GREEK RELIGION

Observance of ritual was the main function of Greek religion and was even more highly revered than the many gods and goddesses of the pantheon, whose behaviour and intervention in human affairs were motivated by emotions such as jealousy, vengeance and lust. Well-established by c.570BCE, the Greek pantheon included major deities such as Apollo, god of healing and music, and Artemis, the chaste goddess of the Moon and the hunt, who were of non-Greek origin. Rituals overseen by priests and priestesses, including dramatic performances at religious festivals, brought the community purpose, especially in hard times. The vast body of mythology included folk heroes left over from pre-Hellenic times, such as Herakles (Hercules).

ANCIENT ROMAN RELIGION

In ancient Rome each deity was responsible for an aspect of daily life and was offered prayer and supplication according to status and necessity. Worship might take place in the home, at a local shrine or sacred place, in a temple or, on feast-days, in a national stadium. The gods were thus "occupational", which made it easy to incorporate foreign deities into the pantheon.

AUSTRALIAN ABORIGINAL BELIEFS

Fundamental to the beliefs of all Aboriginal peoples is the concept of the Dreaming, or Dreamtime – the time when the Sky Heroes or ancestor spirits formed the world and everything in it. Where those spirits left their mark, in unusual features of the local terrain, are the Dreaming tracks or "songlines". It is at the site of these songlines, or through spiritual connection with them, that today's Aborigines can ritually participate in the Dreamtime, especially in relation to the

spirit or animal that is their own tribal totem. Great reverence is paid to such sacred areas, of which the best known in the West is probably Uluru (Ayers Rock). The Aboriginal use of religious symbolism can be seen in their complex artwork and body-painting.

AZTEC RELIGION

The Aztecs' ancestors came from several Central American tribes, all of whom seem to have had a history of being overtaken by severe natural disasters. The result was a strong religious belief that human sacrifice was the only way to avert such disasters in the future. Many of the large number of Aztec deities thus demanded human sacrifice on a regular basis and on an enormous scale. The priests wielded considerable power and possessed an extraordinarily precise calendar which was itself imbued with religious meaning.

BABYLONIAN RELIGION

Babylon was a city-state subject to domination over many centuries by a number of different peoples (including the Sumerians, Assyrians and Persians) who imported their own religious ideas and systems – all of which were duly

African Religions—Babylonian Religion

Babylonian Religion—Gnosticism

incorporated in an extraordinarily diverse pantheon. The main consistent religious sentiment was of reverence for agricultural deities, in particular Tammuz. The great ziggurat, or step pyramid, at Babylon was part of a religious complex dedicated to the chief deity Marduk, god of the spring Sun.

BUDDHISM

The goal of Buddhism is enlightenment – release from the physical and mental attachments of the world, and from the cycle of reincarnation by which one soul is reborn in a succession of different bodies, in order finally to merge with the infinite entity that is the Supreme Self. The first person to attain enlightenment was Siddhartha Gautama, known as the Buddha, in India about 2,500 years ago, and it was he who set out the means by which enlightenment is achievable: the Four Noble Truths and the Eightfold Path. The original form of the religion is known as Theravada; the more evolved and liberal form is called Mahayana, which includes the notion that a *bodhisattva* may delay reaching the final stage of enlightenment in order to inspire others. Other forms of Buddhism

are current in Tibet and Japan. Buddhism requires considerable self-discipline and asceticism and, to some extent, is as much a philosophy or way of life as a religion.

CELTIC BELIEFS

There was never a single Celtic religion: Celtic groups (from *c.*3000BCE onward) revered their various deities on a strictly local and ancestral basis, and with appropriate rites. However, there were certain constant elements. For example, all Celts believed in an afterlife; many of the Celtic gods and goddesses were somehow triple or triune in nature; and there was an unusually high proportion of female deities. Many of the deities were intimately linked with the powers of nature or with the violence of warfare. Another element was a fascination with the idea of magic, especially in association with legendary locations.

CHRISTIANITY

Christians believe that spiritual salvation is possible for all who sincerely believe that Jesus Christ underwent formal execution by Crucifixion to redeem their sins; that he physically rose from the dead two days later; and that he was the Son of God. Whether he was in addition also therefore the Messiah foretold by the prophets of Judaism remains shrouded in mystery, following the formal acceptance by Christian authorities four centuries later of the doctrine propagated by Jesus' major follower, Paul. Paul's doctrine developed the mystical concept of the Trinity: the belief that one God exists in three "Persons", of whom Jesus is one and the Holy Spirit another. Jesus' teachings were inspirational in both spiritual and social terms, but the plethora of differing interpretations over the centuries has led to a considerable diversity of Christian Churches and denominations. Many of these observe different forms of ritual.

CONFUCIANISM

Confucianism is a philosophy of altruism by which people with authority are required to strive for the happiness and wellbeing of those for whom they are responsible, the overall result to aspire to "heavenly" perfection. Confucianism has thus contributed markedly to the social and political order of China for millennia after its institution by Confucius (Kong Fu Zi) in the late 6th century BCE.

DAOISM

The major tenet of Daoism (or Taoism) is that there is a unity behind the multiplicity visible in the world, a connection between human affairs and the events of nature, and an overall balance and harmony in the cycles of life. The central beliefs of Daoism are expressed in the *Dao De Jing*, a book thought to have been written by Lao Zi in the 5th or 6th century BCE. By following the *Dao*, or Way, the devotee can seek spiritual contentment through experiencing oneness with the natural world. The Daoist ideal is *wu wei*, or non-action, a state of contemplation that is not intent upon any result.

GNOSTICISM

This esoteric, mystical form of philosophical faith developed in the Greco-Roman world in the 2nd century CE. It had the greatest influence on the young religion of Christianity, and stressed the redemptive power of esoteric knowledge achieved through divine revelation. The material world was perceived as essentially evil and corrupt. Revelation of human origin, essence and destiny might be achieved only by intuiting the mystery of the self, rather than

Babylonian Religion—Gnosticism

Gnosticism—Mystery Cults

through intellectual study or scriptural reference.

HINDUISM

Intertwined with the history and caste-categorized society of India over millennia, Hinduism propounds that the goal of spirituality is the final merging, after many successive human incarnations, of the individual soul with Ultimate Reality. Such a release (*moksha*) from the cycle of rebirth is attainable primarily through righteous conduct (*dharma*) and by the renunciation of worldly attachments. The Hindu pantheon contains a veritable host of deities. Most Hindus worship one of three: Vishnu, the creator and protector of humankind; Shiva, the destroyer, cosmic dancer and symbol of male energy; or Shakti, the great goddess and female counterpart of Shiva. Rituals and practices vary greatly. Pilgrimage is common, and there are many festivals.

ISLAM

Muslims believe that the words of their holy book, the Koran, are the words of Allah himself, as revealed to the Prophet Muhammad – the latest and greatest of the holy prophets, of which Abraham and

Jesus were earlier exemplars – during the 7th century CE. Considered the unchangeable words of God, they have to be obeyed with submission and precise attention to ritual and ritual purity. A righteous life, or a martyr's death, leads to paradise, often seen as a garden.

JAINISM

Jainism originated in India in the 6th century BCE, around the same time as Buddhism. To Jains, every living being has a spirit or soul, and may, over time, through successive incarnations, progress beyond the human stage, and eventually release itself from the cycle of rebirth and reach *nirvana*. Such potentiality means that all life must be regarded as sacrosanct and all forms of violence shunned. Some Jain ascetics and monks accordingly go naked apart from nose-masks (to avoid breathing in dust-mites), and sweep the ground beneath their feet.

JUDAISM

An ancient religion, dating from the 2nd millennium BCE, Judaism was unusual for its time in being strictly monotheistic. From early on, its adherents, known as Hebrews or Israelites, regarded themselves as the Chosen People of a single God who, by direct contact and through patriarchs and prophets, revealed laws of conduct (notably the Ten Commandments) by which all humankind might in due course – depending on God's judgment on the Last Day – find spiritual salvation. The Hebrew Bible contributed greatly to the traditions of Christianity, and to a lesser extent those of Islam; later writings and commentaries have amounted to a significant body of religious teaching. Orthodox Jews follow an annual schedule of feasts and fasts; rituals are performed both in the home and at the synagogue.

MANICHAEISM

Mani, the founder of Manichaeism (c.240 CE), posited that the world had become invaded by the evil principle. Within an esoteric framework of mythology – including elements of Gnostic Christianity – he declared that the release of goodness into the world would effect not only the original state of separation between good and evil but salvation for all in the resultant Kingdom of Light. Adherents were required to conform to a highly ascetic regime of self-discipline.

MAYAN RELIGION

The Maya (c.300–900CE) were an agricultural civilization in Central America to whom corn (maize) was the most significant crop. The religion thus focused partly on the corn god and other deities responsible for good harvests, and partly on gods inimical to humans and their wellbeing, such as those believed to bring floods. Rituals (including sacrifices) in relation to both benevolent and malign deities were complex. The powerful Mayan priests were highly-skilled astronomers, who made intricate calendrical calculations.

MYSTERY CULTS

This is a general name for those esoteric forms of religious practice during Greco-Roman times that involved highly secret ceremonies to which only initiates were admitted. They include the Eleusinian mysteries (dedicated to Demeter and Persephone), Mithraism (involving the sacrifice of a bull to Mithras, originally a Persian deity) and various rites consecrated to Dionysus. Most incorporated some form of mystical "journey" to the Underworld and back, featuring either total immersion in water or a rite within a dark and cavernous

Gnosticism—Mystery Cults

Mystery Cults–Sikhism

space; re-emergence had connotations of ritual cleansing or the start of a new life. Some additionally held out the promise of a blissful afterlife. Many of the cults were specific to one location or region.

NATIVE NORTH AMERICAN RELIGIONS

Fairly constant among hundreds of overlapping traditions are: reverence for a Great Spirit; thunderbirds – giant birds whose eyes flash lightning and whose wingbeats produce thunder and rain, and yet who are generally benevolent; an Underworld that is basically malevolent but from which the herbs and grasses grow; the essential spirits of animals, birds and major plants who may correspond to tribal or personal totems; and the ancestral spirits of the tribe. Religious ritual is mostly communal (involving dancing and chanting), but for certain ceremonies or divinations may feature a shaman or wise woman.

NEOLITHIC BELIEFS

Neolithic cultures (*c.*8000–3000 BCE) saw the rise of agriculture and settled communities. At the beginning of this time, society was probably matriarchal and the chief deities were accordingly female – the mother goddess, the Sun goddess and the fire goddess – with particular reference to the seasonal fertility of nature and the regular cycles of the female human body. Once armed defence of the settled community became necessary, a change of polarity in the dominant sex both of communal leaders and of deities became observable in most societies.

NORSE BELIEFS

Robust characters for hearty story-telling rather than religious entities, the Norse pantheon of the Vikings (9th–10th centuries) represented deifications of natural forces, of legendary founders of human skills and arts, and of the supposed inaugurators of festivals. But the final warlike gods who dwelt in Asgard, known as the Aesir, were preceded by the more peaceable Vanir. Elements of magic were present, as reflected in its ritual observances. The Vikings believed in an afterlife, known as Valhalla. Kings and outstanding warriors were taken there by the Valkyries (war goddesses) after death. They also conceived an apocalyptic vision of the world's final cataclysm – Ragnarok.

POLYNESIAN BELIEFS

Much of Polynesian mythology (which includes the legends of New Zealand and Hawaii) is concerned with an account of the creation effected by the Sky and the Earth, which between them produced the gods, who in turn created the first woman and the first man. Such creative power is known as *mana*, a term also applied to the social power and influence that equates to rank in human society – a concept that is still of importance, as those of high rank are expected to remain ritually pure and to avoid all that is *tapu* (taboo).

SHAMANISM

Shamanism is a form of religious ritual – engaged in especially by those of animist or totemic beliefs – in which a shaman, usually male, enters a trance and so travels within the spirit world. The object may be to supplicate for a desired worldly benefit (such as a child, a cure, a good harvest, or rain), to placate or pacify a spirit identified as angry or malign, or to discover who is at fault for a crime or injury, particularly a sudden death. Europe and Antarctica are the only two continents in which shamans do not practise regularly.

SHINTO

Shinto – the "way of the gods" (*kami*) – is the ancient indigenous religion of Japan and its tenets permeate the whole of Japanese custom and society. It centres on the belief that the *kami*, who are essentially spirits as much as gods, occupy and control all aspects and workings of nature in the world. Worshippers at the many shrines all over Japan clap their hands once or twice to attract the attention of the *kami* present, before making their supplication or ritual offering. Some Shinto rituals may be practised in the home; others constitute national festivals. Since the 19th century, a number of different Shinto sects have emerged, some of which now have their own large, organized communities.

SIKHISM

Founded in India by Guru Nanak in the 15th century, Sikhism centres on a belief in one transcendent God who saturates the world that he has created. Through successive incarnations – during which the guiding concepts must be work, worship and charity – a human soul may progress to final liberation and become truly God-centred (*gurmukh*) through the

Mystery Cults—Sikhism

grace of God, who is regarded as the ultimate Guru (teacher). A community religion, Sikhism requires formal initiation into the faith and daily ritual worship and observances, although there is no priesthood as such.

SUFISM

Sufism is a highly ascetic Islamic mystical movement popularized first in the 12th century. Organized in the equivalent of monastic orders, each order has its own form of ecstatic worship that generally depends on repetition of either a word or phrase (such as the name of Allah) or of an activity that has the same connotations (such as the whirling of the Mevlevi dervishes). In modern times, some orders have allowed degrees of congregational participation.

SUMERIAN RELIGION

As befits the faith of a very early civilization (*c.*3000–2550BCE), most of the Sumerians' religious beliefs were directed toward general security and daily wellbeing – the main deities were those of the natural (elemental) forces, of agricultural and domestic fertility, and of victory in war. Great temples and towers were built to house the worshippers and their rites, although the tutelary deities might differ in each city-state. That worshippers believed that even their greatest kings were subject to divine will is evident from the figure of the legendary hero Gilgamesh, whose attempts to find immortality are frustrated by the gods.

TANTRISM

Tantra, or Tantrism, is the use of certain esoteric practices – forms of meditation, including yoga – to achieve a state of spiritual and physical ecstasy. Applied in some denominations of Hinduism and Buddhism, Tantrism features *yantras* (mystical diagrams) and *mantras* (mystical repetitions or formulae). Hindu Tantra may involve sexual intercourse as a means of attaining enlightenment. Buddhist Tantrism usually stipulates the presence of a *guru* (instructor).

VEDIC RELIGION

The Aryans who invaded India during the 2nd millennium BCE carried with them the *Vedas*, their sacred texts – a vast compilation, in Sanskrit, of philosophy and liturgy, most of it in verse. A large proportion deals with several creation myths, featuring some of the gods that remain important in modern Hinduism and others that have now faded into relative obscurity – such as Indra, Agni and Varuna. The stories have much to do with the physical and military difficulties of the Aryan invasion, but the *Vedas* remain sacred to Hindus today as the historical basis of their beliefs.

VOODOO

Basically a form of shamanism, Voodoo combines African and Christian religious elements and animism – its gods include deities from West Africa, Christian saints, and the spirits of natural forces and ancestors. Voodoo is prevalent in Haiti in the West Indies, although similar practices occur in some parts of northern South America. At almost all Voodoo ceremonies – after prior permission is obtained from the "gateway god" Legba – the shaman and one or more of the worshippers enter a trance and are possessed by one of the gods, taking on the deity's characteristics.

ZEN BUDDHISM

Zen is a monastic tradition of Buddhism which entered Japan from China in the 12th century. It stresses the personal experience of enlightenment through meditation and a simple life lived close to nature. There are two main strands of Zen in Japan: Rinzai Zen, which seeks sudden and spontaneous enlightenment (often through the medium of a *koan*, or impossible conundrum, posed by a teacher); and Soto Zen, in which the achieving of enlightenment is a more gradual process through *zazen*, or "sitting meditation".

ZOROASTRIANISM

In Persia (now Iran) *c.*1000BCE, the religious philosopher Zoroaster (Zarathustra) created a new system of faith from the religious elements of his time. One of the earliest instances of monotheism, the new religion was dualist in nature, pitting the great creator god, Ahura Mazda, against the evil Hostile Spirit, Angra Mainyu, who in the fullness of time was finally to be vanquished. Zoroastrianism still has a number of followers today. It is a community religion in which the priesthood is hereditary; communal daily prayers are required; other rites take place in the home or may be solemnized in a temple, which gives a sacred fire pride of place.

Sikhism—Zoroastrianism

INDEX

Index

Index

ACKNOWLEDGMENTS

The publishers wish to thank the following photographers and organizations for their kind permission to reproduce the copyright material in this book.

KEY: t: top, b: bottom, c: centre, l: left, r: right

AA&A: Ancient Art and Architecture, Pinner
AKG: Archiv für Kunst und Geschichte, London
BAL: Bridgeman Art Library, London
BL: British Library, London
BM: British Museum, London
TSI: Tony Stone Images, London
V&A: Victoria and Albert Museum, London
WFA: Werner Forman Archive, London

Page 11 BAL/BL; **12** V&A; **13** Hutchison Library; **14** V&A; **21** Art Archive; **22** Biblioteca Apostolica Vaticana; **24** Art Archive; **26** Art Archive; **28** BM; **31** Michael Holford; **32** Zefa; **33** Art Archive/V&A; **36** WFA/BM; **37** BAL; **40** DBP Archive; **43** BM; **44** Art Archive; **46** Art Archive; **48** Elizabeth Whiting; **53** Art Archive; **54** Norma Joseph/Royal Geographical Society; **56** Pictorial Press of China/DBP Archive; **58** AA&A; **60** BAL/BM; **62** BAL/Bibliothèque Royale de Belgique; **63l** Christie's Images; **63r** DBP Archive; **64** BAL/Musée Guimet; **65** Jurgen Liepe; **66** DBP Archive; **67t** Michael Holford; **67b** Hutchison Library; **70** Scala; **71** BAL; **74** BM; **80** BM; **81** Paul Harris/Royal Geographical Society; **83** BAL; **85** BAL; **88–89** BAL/V&A; **93** Michael Holford; **95** Art Archive/Chavez Ballon Collection; **96** BAL/Bibliothèque Nationale, Paris; **97** Scala; **99** Superstock Fine Arts; **100** Private Collection; **103** AA&A; **104** BAL/Monasterio de El Escorial; **107** Graham Harrison; **108** Glen Allison/TSI; **109** BM; **110** BAL/San Tomé, Toledo; **111** BAL/BL; **113t** Mary Evans Picture Library; **113b** Michael Holford/BM; **114b, 114t** Michael Holford; **115** Michael Holford; **116b** BM; **116t** Scala/Museo Gregorino Egizio, Vatican; **117** National Gallery, London; **120** BL; **121** Ohio Historical Society, Ohio; **122** BAL/Oriental Museum, University of Durham; **123** WFA; **124** Scala/Museo Nazionale, Naples; **126** J. Holmes/Panos Pictures; **127** BM; **129** Hutchison Library; **132** Art Archive/National Gallery of Mexico; **133** Art Archive/Palazzo Barbarini, Rome; **134** Charles Walker Collection; **136** Mick Sharp Photography; **139** Art Archive/Museum of Archaeology, Naples; **141** Hutchison Library; **142** Charles Walker Collection; **143** Hutchison Library; **144t** AKG/Royal Library, Copenhagen; **145t** Paul Harris/Royal Geographical Society; **145b** John Bigelow Taylor; **147** BL; **149** BAL/Louvre, Paris; **150–151** Hutchison Library;

151 Corbis/Smithsonian Institution; **152** Charles Walker Collection; **153** Michael Holford; **154** Art Archive/Monasterio de El Escorial; **154–155** BL (OR 2668 f.2v); **157b** DBP Archive; **157t** BL (Add. 11695 f240); **158** Michael Holford/BM; **159** BAL/Oriental Museum, University of Durham; **160** BAL; **161b** AA&A; **161t** Robert Harding Picture Library; **164** DBP Archive; **165** C.M. Dixon; **166** BAL/V&A; **167** BAL/Museo Diocesana, Cortona; **168** BAL/Louvre, Paris; **169** BAL/Albright-Knox Gallery, Buffalo; **171** Art Archive/National Gallery, London; **172** Superstock Fine Arts; **173** DBP Archive; **174** BL (Add. 47672 f170); **176** WFA/National Gallery, Prague; **178–179** BAL; **180b, 180t** DBP Archive; **183** Julian Rothenstein Collection; **184–185** Scala/Museo Paestum; **186** Art Archive; **186–187** Art Archive/Royal Fine Arts Museum, Antwerp; **188** Art Archive/Anagni Cathedral; **189** BAL/Dora Holzhandler; **190** DBP/Wat Buddhapadipa, London; **191** BAL/BL; **192** BAL; **193** Art Archive; **194** Mary Evans Picture Library; **195** BL (Or641 f267r); **198** Hutchison Library; **199** BAL/Scrovegni Chapel, Padua; **202** Art Archive/Scrovegni Chapel, Padua; **204** Jean-Leo Dugast/Panos Pictures; **206** BAL/Palazzo Bianco, Genoa; **206–207** Bodleian Library, Oxford (Ms Ouseley Add. 171.b.f4v); **208–209** Art Archive; **209** DBP Archive; **211** DBP Archive; **212–213** BL (Add. Or1814); **216** BM; **217** BL; **219** AKG/Mount Athos Monastery; **220** Art Archive; **221** BAL/BL; **222** Piers Vitebsky; **223** WFA/Philip Goldman Collection; **224** Hutchison Library; **227** BAL; **229** BAL/Jean-Loup Charmet; **230** BAL/Fitzwilliam Museum, Cambridge; **230–231** AA&A; **234–235** BAL/Dora Holzhandler; **236–237** BAL/BL; **238** Art Archive; **239** Art Archive; **240–241** BAL; **246t** Michael Holford/BM; **246b** Ann & Bury Peerless; **247** AKG/Library of Trinity College, Dublin; **248t** BAL; **248b** Michael Holford; **249t** AKG; **249b** Art Archive; **250** Scala; **251** Ann & Bury Peerless; **252t** WFA; **252b** Art Archive; **253** BL (Kings I f.F21); **254–255** BL (Add. 54782 f131v); **255b** Art Archive.

COMMISSIONED ARTWORK CREDITS
Matthew Cooper: 8–9, 15, 69, 119, 163, 190–191, 197, 244–245; *Alison Barrett*: 34, 42–43, 50, 51, 60b, 78, 82–83, 112t, 114bl, 117r, 146t, 149l, 150, 152tr, 152c, 152b, 153r, 158bl, 201, 205, 232–233, 251r; *Louisa St Pierre*: 1, 2, 16, 27, 29, 36–37t, 38–39t, 59b, 61, 65b, 73, 87, 92, 101, 112b, 114t, 116c, 131, 140, 148t, 148b, 155t, 156r, 161t, 181, 214, 225r; *Hannah Fermin*: 76.

The publishers would also like to thank Liz Cowen, Susan Martineau and Mike Darton for their contributions to the book.